CONTEMPORARY
FLORAL
DESIGN

JUDITH BLACKLOCK

The Flower Press

Published by
The Flower Press Ltd
3 East Avenue
Bournemouth
BH3 7BW

First published in 2015

A CIP catalogue record for this book is available from the
British Library.

ISBN-13: 978-0-9552391-9-9

Design: Amanda Hawkes

Printed and bound in China by
C & C Offset Printing Co., Ltd.

CONTENTS

Over the past 50 years there have been a great many developments and innovations in the field of floral design. The Web, Facebook, Instagram and other forms of communication have enabled us to look at, admire and copy or adapt the ideas of inspirational designers and take them to a different level. New products have become available which are being used as accessories to add impact and interest to floral designs. Well-established products have been rediscovered and are being used in new ways. Styles and techniques have evolved, taking the world of flowers ever forward. Most importantly, though, it is the extensive range of beautiful flowers and foliage now available from all parts of the globe that lies at the heart of the designers' inspired work.

As the book's title makes clear, the designs here are all contemporary – that is, they are of the moment. But that does not mean they ignore the classic elements and principles of design. I have had the very great pleasure of bringing together work by the best designers worldwide to create a book that encapsulates the look, feel and style of today's floral design.

JUDITH BLACKLOCK

INTRODUCTION

Contemporary and classic – what is the difference?

CONTEMPORARY

The term 'contemporary' means belonging to the present – it's as simple as that. So this book looks at the inspiration behind the work of top international floral designers at the beginning of the 21st century.

CLASSIC

The term 'classic' is used to refer to floral design that has stood the test of time and continues to be favoured by many as the benchmark for the highest standards. The classic elements and principles of design are constantly referred to by designers today. A similar term, 'traditional', is more limited in scope, referring to design that has been passed down from generation to generation and remains popular in a particular part of the world. Consequently, classic rather than traditional is the term used in this book.

Characteristics of contemporary design

Any study of the best in contemporary design over the past decade will show the emergence and enjoyment of the following characteristics, although obviously this list is not exhaustive:

- a focal area that can be singular or multiple and is not in a set position
- an orderly massing/grouping of plant material
- a pleasing balance, both actual and visual, whether it is symmetric or asymmetric
- exciting and unusual textural contrasts
- the use of only one type of flower or a limited palette of flowers and foliage
- the incorporation of house plant, subtropical and tropical foliage for their bold form and long-lasting qualities
- designs without foliage
- the use of manipulated plant material
- varied and exciting mechanics that are often visible and form part of the design
- containers made from natural plant material
- structures made from natural plant material so that only minimal fresh plant material is needed to create good design
- bold feature flowers such as *Anthurium* and *Hydrangea*
- accessories such as wool, cable ties and perspex

Characteristics of classic design

Classic design is still enjoyed today and can be recognised by some or all of the following characteristics:

- scattered plant material radiating from a common point
- focal or dominant area(s) located two-thirds of the way down from the tip of the tallest stem
- soft and gentle contrasts
- colour, form and texture 'woven' into the design to lead the eye gently through
- space between each element of plant material to show each form to its best advantage
- extensive use of garden foliage
- chicken wire, foam and pin holders often used as mechanics
- containers often made of pottery, porcelain or china
- plastic containers frequently used but hidden by plant material

Note: Of course there can be, and indeed often is, crossover.

Contemporary
This bridal bouquet design is based on colour and texture. The different heights and textures of the *Gloriosa superba* 'Rothschildiana', *Vanda* orchids and *Skimmia* create depth and the bare stems of *Jasminum* break up the stiffness of the leaves, adding movement.

Classic

The beautiful rich colours in this shower bouquet make for dramatic contrasts and dynamic flow. *Rosa* 'Miss Piggy' gives a soft and voluptuous feel, while the *Gloriosa superba* 'Rothschildiana' contrasts wonderfully in colour and texture. Delicate *Genista* (broom) is perfect for more gentle movement. This classic design is so timeless it can also be seen as contemporary.

BELOW **Classic**
Vibrant flowers and Christmas baubles were woven through a classic circle created on a foam base to form this rich, colourful melange.

RIGHT **Contemporary**
An intricate shape, cut from a large sheet of polystyrene, was wrapped round with tape to make it stronger. Plastic tubes were glued to the shape, which was then covered with *Prunus* bark. *Vanda* orchids and grasses were inserted in the tubes to create a contemporary circular design.

ABOVE Classic
The colours may be similar but in this design a wealth of beautiful plant material has been scattered throughout, with space left between the flowers so that each bloom remains distinct.

RIGHT Contemporary
Using contemporary techniques, *Rosa* and *Chrysanthemum* 'Kermit' were massed and *Phalaenopsis* orchids grouped to give strong visual impact.

THE CONCLUSION
OF ALL THINGES
IS TO FEARE GOD
AND KEEPE HIS
COMMAVNDEMENTES

15 E 97

Classic

This table setting incorporates
traditional garden plant material in
elegant containers. The radiation of
the stems from a central point in
each placement provides gracious,
rhythmic movement.

Contemporary

Contemporary techniques and materials have been combined with natural plant material to create an opulent table setting. In the tall glass vases squares of birch bark were topped with spheres of gold-glazed orchid roots. Ceramic vases were filled with spheres of *Hydrangea*, bands of conkers and branches of *Celastrus*. Square metal containers were mixed with gold-rimmed porcelain and crystal glasses containing beautiful *Rosa* 'Cherry Brandy', *Phalaenopsis* 'Kaleidoscope' and *Vanda* orchids, and *Gloriosa* 'Leonella'. Above the table is a canopy of *Fagus sylvatica* 'Purpurea' (copper beech), with hanging *Gloriosa* 'Leonella'. Garlands of *Physalis* (Chinese lantern), conkers, ribbon, berries, beads and autumn leaves decorate the chairs. Neill Strain has created a veritable feast for the eyes here.

Plant material often used in contemporary design

This list is by no means exhaustive, but it includes some of the most popular flowers and foliage that are used in contemporary work and illustrated in the following pages:

- vintage flowers
- fragrant flowers
- seasonal flowers
- preserved plant material
- succulents
- *Anthurium*
- *Chrysanthemum*
- *Cornus* (dogwood)
- *Dahlia*
- *Delphinium*
- *Dianthus* (carnation)
- *Gerbera*
- *Gloriosa superba* 'Rothschildiana'
- *Hippeastrum* (amaryllis)
- *Hydrangea*
- *Leucobryum* (bun moss)
- *Phalaenopsis* orchids
- *Pinus* (pine)
- *Rosa* (modern and old-fashioned varieties)
- *Schoenus* (flexi grass)
- *Vanda* orchids
- *Xanthorrhoea* (steel grass)
- *Xerophyllum tenax* (bear grass)
- *Zantedeschia* (calla)

RIGHT **Fragrant flowers**
Multi-petalled old-fashioned garden roses have been combined with blackberries in an organic container made from woody stems.

ABOVE AND BELOW
Seasonal flowers
A fragrant mix of *Convallaria* (lily of the valley), *Narcissus* and *Syringa* (lilac) – a feast for the senses!

RIGHT **Vintage flowers**
Lace fabric and ribbon create a vintage feel, using soft muted colours with a touch of pure white.

ABOVE **Vintage flowers**
Roses that are fragrant or have muted colours are considered vintage and are fashionable for all occasions. Here *Rosa* 'Memory Lane' is combined with *Heuchera* leaves in a 1930s container.

LEFT *Chrysanthemum*
Fifteen thousand heads of *Chrysanthemum* were used to create these floral diamonds, each of which was made with two cones, one up-ended, which were tightly bound with tape and impaled on a metal spike.

RIGHT **Seasonal flowers**
Paeonia (peony) and *Prunus serrulata* (cherry blossom) are seasonal favourites.

Anthurium

Anthurium, which is available in a wide range of colours, shapes and sizes, is admired for its longevity and the sculptural form of its spathe and spadix.

Vanda
A floral heart featuring gorgeous *Vanda* 'Divana® Pink Mahogany'.

LEFT Succulents
Rosettes of *Sempervivum* and *Echeveria* create wonderful textural contrast in this design for spring.

RIGHT Succulents
This group of succulent rosettes sitting comfortably in a natural landscape makes it clear that flowers are not always necessary for effective and attractive contemporary design.

Dahlia
Two beautiful *Dahlia*
were all that was
needed in this low glass
bowl surrounded by
swirls and stapled coils
of flat cane.

Plant material often used in contemporary design

Preserved plant material
The grey furry texture of preserved *Stachys byzantina* leaves is enjoyed by many designers. Here the leaves have been glued to an inexpensive container which was then filled with fresh orchids.

LEFT *Hippeastrum*
With their bold form, *Hippeastrum* (amaryllis) are loved by designers. Here they are displayed in an unconventional contemporary manner in a wet floral sphere. The sputnik of flowers has been created with bleached sticks, blue spruce, festive baubles and, of course, amaryllis.

RIGHT *Zantedeschia*
Available in a range of luscious colours, *Zantedeschia* (calla) will provide bold structural form in design work. Here *Zantedeschia* 'Schwarzwalder' have been combined with rolled and wired *Cycas revoluta* (sago palm) leaves and wired *Equisetum* (snake grass) stems at complementary angles.

LEFT *Cornus*
Cornus (dogwood) creates additional interest in this table setting featuring *Rosa* 'Green Eye' and *Dendrobium* (Singapore orchid). Whether bound or woven, the smooth texture and beautiful colours of *Cornus* are always interesting in floral design work.

Pinus

Delicate, vertical placements of *Pinus* (pine) needles are supported by intertwined wire and decorated with trails of *Senecio rowleyanus* (pea plant) and *Eucharis* (Amazon lily) in glass tubes.

ABOVE *Leucobryum*
Cut tufts of *Leucobryum* (bun moss) have been inserted into a foam base to create a spiral movement, while *Plagiothecium* (flat moss) provides subtle contrast. Star-like *Ornithogalum arabicum* (chincherinchee) give contrast of colour and form. *Hypericum* berries have been dotted through the design.

RIGHT *Delphinium*
The stunning *Delphinium* is a popular flower in the summer months. Here a framework of bare branches gives support and adds volume to the design. Individual flowers attached with thin wire to the branches extend the sweep of blue colour.

Vanda
Vanda 'Kanchana®
Magic Blue' is probably
the most popular *Vanda*
because of its wonderful
distinctive colour.

BELOW *Xerophyllum tenax*
BELOW *Xerophyllum tenax*
A wave of *Xerophyllum tenax* (bear grass) features in
this waterfall design, with *Narcissus* buds and *Primula
vulgaris* (primrose) on a bed of moss adding interest.

RIGHT *Xanthorrhoea*
Gloriosa superba
'Rothschildiana' provide
simple but effective
impact in a design of three
cylinder vases. Double-
sided tape was wrapped
round the containers,
which were then covered
with strands of
Xanthorrhoea (steel grass).

ABOVE *Schoenus*
Easy to bend and smooth-textured, *Schoenus* (flexi grass) is ideal for creating space and movement. Here it encircles a slim, elegant conical design.

RIGHT *Phalaenopsis* **orchids**
Long-lasting cut stems of *Phalaenopsis* orchids are combined with *Sticherus* (umbrella fern). *Phalaenopsis* is beautiful as both a pot plant and a cut flower.

Rosa
The petals and flowers of
7,000 *Rosa* 'Pearl
Avalanche' by John Meijer
were used to decorate tall
'umbrella' metal
constructions reinforced
with *Cornus* (dogwood).
The base was covered
with foam and then moss.

Dianthus

The ubiquitous *Dianthus* (carnation) becomes a designer flower when cut short, massed, grouped or used individually in a novel way. Here paper parcels, hanging on twine, hold bloom and spray flowers.

Hydrangea

Hydrangea is loved by flower designers for both contemporary and classic work. The bold form and size of the blooms make them a must in large-scale designs.

LEFT *Gerbera*
Gerbera and the smaller mini *Gerbera* offer an incredible range of colours. Their bold, eye-catching form and size make them perfect to work with in many areas of contemporary floral design. Here mini *Gerbera* are combined with *Camellia* and *Ranunculus*.

RIGHT *Gloriosa*
Gloriosa superba 'Rothschildiana' have been wrapped round two impressive huge *Salix* (willow) structures.

Decorative mechanics

Mechanics is the word used to describe supports that keep plant material in position. The range of exposed, decorative mechanics expands with every demonstration given and every book produced. The list that follows includes some that are used frequently in contemporary floral design:

- bark, branches and roots
- cane and sticks
- cork
- fabric
- güllaç
- metal
- mini glass jugs
- orchid tubes
- pegs
- recycled material
- seahorse glass containers
- skeletonised leaves
- twine and fibres such as wool and sisal
- wax
- wire such as aluminium, bullion, stub and mesh

RIGHT **Recycled material**
Polystyrene cups cover three styrofoam spheres in different sizes. Long-lasting floral material – succulents, *Dianthus* (carnation) and trails of *Tradescantia* – was fixed inside the cups.

Aluminium wire
The flowing multiple arms of this construction are made of heavy aluminium wire. Light aluminium wire supports mini glass 'seahorse' containers holding exquisite *Phalaenopsis* orchids. Hanging *Heliconia* create a strong base at the foot of the design.

ABOVE Aluminium wire
Lengths of red aluminium wire decorated with stars were wrapped round a metal ring covered in sisal and placed on a vase. A garland of *Cornus* (dogwood) was added. Tubes were attached, filled with *Gloriosa*, *Gleichenia polypodioides* (coral fern) and larch cones.

BELOW Bullion wire
Coiled circles of bullion wire, framed by *Galax* leaves, support a single pink rose. *Kalanchoe* flower heads, linked by colour and regular placement, provide decorative detail.

LEFT Stub wire
A cascade of *Gloriosa* and berries supported by long heavy-gauge stub wires radiates from a central post.

Stub wire
Heavy-gauge stub wire has been hammered into a plank of wood to provide support for decorative bark, berries and flowers. The wires have not been fully covered because they form part of the design, as does the space between the verticals.

LEFT Wire mesh
Squared wire mesh holds
bleached flat cane,
creating an innovative
structure to support the
much-maligned spray
Dianthus (carnation) and
make it look magnificent.

RIGHT Wire mesh
Decorative, handmade
wire mesh encases a
mass of *Hydrangea*, while
Liriope (lily grass), trails
of *Passiflora* (passion
flower) and summer
flowers give fine detail.

Wire mesh/glass tubes
A sheet of wire mesh held vertical by a metal stand supports test tubes filled with *Astrantia*, *Clematis*, *Zantedeschia* (calla) and loops of *Schoenus* (flexi grass).

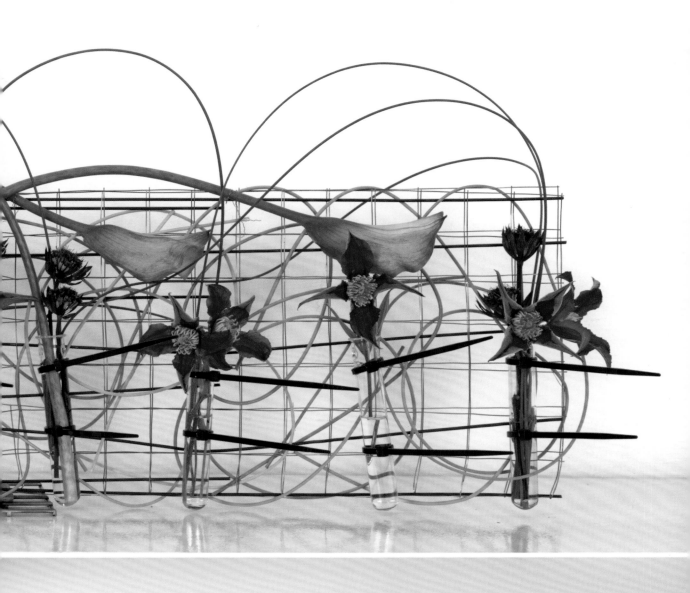

Cork
Two layers of thin cork
support roses, woody
stems, grasses and *Physalis
alkekengi var.* 'Franchetii'
(Chinese lantern).

Wood
Branches secured with
aluminium wire on a
concrete base support
seahorse glass tubes for
Narcissus and *Tulipa*.

ABOVE Bark
Bark squares have been linked together to
create pockets for *Phalaenopsis* orchid plants
and trailing *Amaranthus*.

RIGHT Branches and roots
Branches and roots provide vertical interest and
texture as well as giving support to a mix of colourful
summer flowers.

LEFT AND ABOVE
Cane/orchid tubes
Bambusa (bamboo) and
twiggy branches disguise
the metal supports helping
to keep this structure
stable. The branches hold
tubes containing a mix of
colourful flowers.

RIGHT Cane
The swirling cane collar ties in perfectly with the extension and supports *Vanda* 'Blue Magic', *Humulus* (hop) and stripped *Stephanotis* trails.

ABOVE Sticks
Flexible midelino sticks provide both decoration at the top of the container and a mechanic that supports the flowers.

LEFT Cane
Horizontal strips of cane support *Dianthus* (carnation) in mini glass bottles.

RIGHT Seahorse glass containers
Yellow cable ties hold together a structure of *Cornus* (dogwood) on which mini glass seahorses holding *Anemone* and *Ranunculus* have been hung.

Orchid tubes
Plastic orchid tubes have
been covered with raffia
and then fixed in place
with twisted paper-covered
wire (bind wire). They were
filled with *Diplocyclos*,
Lunaria annua (honesty),
Panicum virgatum
(fountain grass),
Sandersonia and
Vanda orchids.

ABOVE **Metal**
A metal construction supports spheres of vibrant
Gerbera, while a flourish of *Xerophyllum tenax* (bear
grass) adds detail.

ABOVE Güllaç
Sheets of güllaç (wafers made from cornflour and wheat flour used in Middle Eastern cookery) were glued in layers to a V-shaped construction of chicken wire strengthened with tape. The base of the V was covered in plastic to allow for the placement of wet foam and some beautiful summer flowers and grasses. Note that güllaç hates contact with water!

RIGHT Wax
Sheets of paraffin wax were made in a wax-melting machine, then branches and *Pinus* (pine) needles were added. The sheets were placed vertically in a wax container and tubes containing *Eucharis* (Amazon lily) were inserted between them.

Twine
In an innovative twist, spring flowers have been inserted into the centre of spools of twine, which give support.

LEFT Skeletonised leaves
Skeletonised leaves,
both natural and
coloured, offer a
translucent textural
contrast.

RIGHT Fabric
The base of this design
is a foam sphere to which
texture has been added
by gluing on torn strips of
mousseline fabric ribbon.
The ribbon has then been
threaded through the
vertical stems, which have
their ends in the foam.

LEFT Recycled material
Plastic bags filled with
recycled bubble wrap and
water-absorbing gel have
been placed on a metal
ring bound with wool.
A single rose was inserted
in each bag.

RIGHT Twine
Twine has been criss-
crossed over and around
a simple container to
provide support for the
flowers, which can be
easily replaced with the
mechanics retained.

Pegs
A design of clothes pegs and *Vanda* 'Black Magic' orchids. The pegs are bound to a palisade with silver aluminium wire.

Recycled material
Skilfully cut egg cartons were
reassembled to provide an
interesting support for a few
heads of *Vanda* orchids.

Recycled material
The 'eternal triangle'
design was created from
linked triangles of various
sizes made from
insulation board covered
with old newspaper.
About 150 triangles were
used, each one lined with
flower heads.

RIGHT **Recycled material**
A tall plastic plant pot
was lined with black
polythene and covered in
recycled wrapping paper
glued at the sides with
PVA, then filled with
Rosa 'Vuvuzela' and
Kalanchoe, together with
Choisya foliage and silver
Brunia.

ABOVE **Recycled material**
Disused post bags,
suspended from strong
rope, have been recycled
to create innovative
containers for *Anthurium*.

RIGHT **Recycled material**
The recycled fishing net
and rope, with their
subdued colour and
texture, provide the
perfect foil to *Lilium* (lily)
and *Anthurium*.

Accessories

An accessory is something added to make the design more interesting or attractive. It does not necessarily have to be non-vegetative and the options are obviously limitless. The following list gives some of the more widely used examples:

- buttons
- candles
- decorative wire
- fabric and leather
- fruits, beans and vegetables
- glass, perspex and Plexiglas
- rattan and raffia
- reeds, sticks, stems and roots
- ribbon, feathers and beads
- shells, natural sponge and sea kelp
- sisal and coconut fibre
- stones and coal
- wood and pegs
- wool, felted wool, string and twine

RIGHT **Perspex**
Hanging lengths of perspex form an important part of this stunning window hanging. *Hypericum* berries threaded on *Schoenus* (flexi grass), together with orchids and skeletonised leaves, complete the design.

Fabric
Brightly coloured fabric with a dominant pattern plays an important part in this extravagant table design. The flowers need to be strong, bold and equally colourful so as not to be overwhelmed.

String
Inflated balloons were part-wrapped with string, which was then covered with a textile hardener such as Paverpol. Once that had dried, the balloons were deflated and removed. Foam was inserted in the resulting 'nests', while slices of bleached mulberry bark were placed between them to create linkage. White *Phalaenopsis* orchid blooms and *Ceropegia* vine provide the decorative plant material, together with wrapped *Corylus* (hazel) twigs.

LEFT AND RIGHT Leather
Leather soaked in tea gives accent and interesting texture here, its subtle colour linking harmoniously with *Hydrangea* 'Rodeo Classic' and Florigene *Dianthus* (carnation). Mixed foliage, including *Xerophyllum tenax* (bear grass), *Xanthorrhoea* (steel grass) and *Aspidistra*, was woven into an archway constructed from heavy metal rods.

Coconut fibre
Coconut fibre has been bound onto disposable plastic tubes with decorative wire.

Vegetables
A mass of black-eyed peas encircle a design of *Hippeastrum* (amaryllis). Pastilles of wool provide textural interest.

LEFT Fruits
Fruits and vegetables have wonderful colour, form and texture. Here the shiny surface of the pomegranates complements the subdued paper-covered polystyrene, especially when linked to the soft-textured *Rosa* 'Pacific Blue'. Contrast of form and texture is particularly important in monochromatic colour schemes.

RIGHT Vegetables
Leeks surround a cut-down water bottle with rose hips placed inside. In the small arrangements colourful leaves were pinned to foam into which spray roses were then inserted.

Vegetables
A ring of buoyant potatoes
supports an intricate
structure of twigs to
which tubes containing
Gloriosa superba
'Rothschildiana' have
been attached.

LEFT Vegetables
In this naturalistic composition flowers are subsidiary to the bark and mushrooms but together they create a pleasing whole.

RIGHT Decorative wire
Aluminium wire has been used to attach plastic tubes covered with *Galax* leaves to glittered birch twigs in order to create an alternative Christmas tree.

Sticks
The use of midelino sticks was important in this design
by Rudy Casati, who created a 'fluctuating book living
off hundreds of flying letters, free to go round the world'
as a special exhibit in one of the Oxford colleges.
Eighty low, square, water-filled containers were placed
on a table to form a continuous line. Countless wires
were first attached to chicken wire that had been
placed over the containers and then taken to points
high and low around the room.

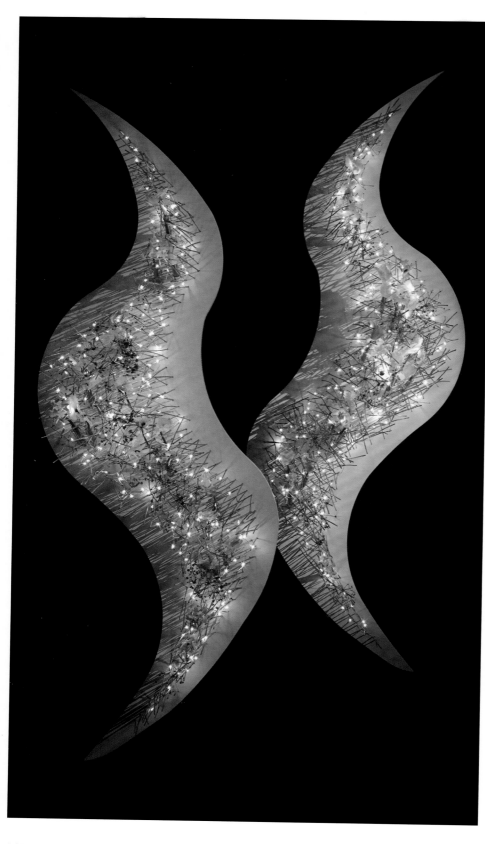

LEFT Reeds
Reeds were inserted in shapes cut from foam. Glass tubes containing *Cyclamen* were then tied to the structure and dried seed heads and lights were scattered through.

RIGHT Sticks
Sticks are fundamental here, catching the eye with their neutral colouring and intricate texture.

Reeds
Mikado stems (natural
reeds) were used to create
a fan-like structure.
A drift of plant material
was then attached, to
create a second focus
within the design.

LEFT Stems
The strong vertical form created by the mitsumata branches repeats the line of the rectangular container and gives support to the plant material.

RIGHT Stems
A magnificent mix of glorious summer flowers – double lilies, *Gerbera* and *Antirrhinum* – in a fish bowl, all linked with trails of stripped stems.

Roots
Vanda orchid roots are frequently used in contemporary work for their sinuous form.

Wool
Cones wrapped in coloured wool provide decorative containers for *Gerbera* against a backdrop of *Aspidistra* leaves where the stems have been detached and superimposed over the leaves.

BELOW Wool
LEHNER Wolle[3]
Woolcords provide a wonderful contrast to the smooth texture of the apples and roses.

RIGHT Felted wool/ribbon
The combination of LEHNER Wolle[3] Lunte and vintage ribbon gives subtle textural contrast and complements the colours of the plant material. Lunte is very soft and covers containers inexpensively to give an exciting new look.

LEFT   Felted wool
The centres of colourful coils of LEHNER Wolle[3] felted wool support glass tubes into which tulips have been placed.

ABOVE AND RIGHT   Wool
Decorative wool has been bound over long, heavy-gauge stub wires to provide interesting texture in this hanging design featuring *Gloriosa*, *Tillandsia* (air plant), *Paphiopedilum* (slipper orchid) and spider-like *Brassia* orchids.

String
One of the main features of this star-shaped design is the form created from the crocheted and knitted string which complements the layered petals and dried seed

Twine has been criss-crossed over and around a simple
container to provide support for the flowers and
decorative detail.

RIGHT **Twine**
The 'petals' created by the metalwork frame were
covered with double-sided tape and green garden twine.
Coils were adhered to the petals for detail. The large
'flower' was held in place with a base plate and central
screw fixed to a wrought-iron cross. A wreath ring was
glued to the base for the flowers.

Rattan
Strips of rattan were tied into a construction created from aluminium wire. Stems were then inserted through, with additional flowers being attached with lengths of rattan to give a perfect domed shape.

LEFT Raffia
Coloured raffia was used to decorate a construction of chicken wire that had been sprayed red. *Anthurium* and *Gloriosa superba* 'Rothschildiana' were added to complement the colour scheme, together with trails of *Passiflora* (passion flower) and *Diplocyclos*.

ABOVE Ribbon
Ribbon is an integral part of this table design. The colours have been chosen to match the *Gloriosa superba* 'Rothschildiana' in pink, yellow and orange, alongside an exciting new variety of *Gerbera, G.* 'Pasta Pennoni' (spaghetti gerbera), and fresh strawberries, apples and redcurrants.

Ribbon
Sumptuous satin ribbon is linked to the felted wool to give textural contrast.

Feathers
A cloud of feathers provides a beautiful romantic backdrop for the David Austin roses in this irresistible hand-tied bouquet by Per Benjamin, created on a handmade wire structure.

The soft, downy texture of the feathers contrasts beautifully with the strength of the surrounding coils of bleached willow. *Nerine* in tubes complete the picture.

Full of energy and rhythmic dynamism, *The Sun* – a tree of glass created by Dale Chihuly – has not a flower in sight. My only excuse is that I love it and it is, after all, firmly embedded in a sea of green leaves!

Beads
Beads threaded on wire surround a column of coloured sticks to create a decorative container holding *Anigozanthos* (kangaroo paw) and roses.

LEFT Glass
Small glass bottles, each filled with a single bloom of *Vanda* orchid, look charming suspended through trailing *Xerophyllum tenax* (bear grass). Dynamism is created through repetition.

RIGHT Glass
Fine twisted strands of glass, complemented by *Sempervivum* at the base, are highlighted by a few heads of *Vanda* orchid.

ABOVE AND BELOW Glass
Glass tubes suspended on a bold metal construction hold *Anthurium*, *Gloriosa* and *Hypericum*, with blackberries and pleated, threaded sections of *Aspidistra* leaf.

LEFT **Perspex**
For this 'enchanted forest' 2,000 long branches were joined together with black wire. Their ends were supported in 160 compartmentalised low perspex dishes, abutting each other to create a rectangle. *Astilbe*, *Amaranthus caudatus*, *Physalis* and *Astrantia* were placed in glass tubes and suspended from the branches. Magical, brightly coloured leaves were created by placing *Liquidambar* and *Magnolia* leaves between plastic sheets and laminating them. The sheets were then cut into geometric shapes and the perspex dishes filled with water of different colours.

ABOVE **Wood**
Pinus (pine) needles were inserted individually through perforations in a perspex sheet that was supported at the corners by blocks of wood, giving additional interest through their contrasting colour, form and texture.

Plexiglas

Plexiglas and heavy-duty aluminium wire have been manipulated to create a structure which supports and enhances a few bold flowers and a minimal amount of foliage. *Schoenus* (flexi grass) creates enclosed space.

ABOVE Shells
Rosa, *Phalaenopsis*
orchids and *Agapanthus*
have been combined with
textured sea urchin shells
in a square container
constructed from OASIS®
Bindwire and rolled
Populus alba (silver
poplar) leaves.

RIGHT Coal
Washed coal has been
glued piece by piece to
three MDF shapes with
black silicone, then
sprayed with silver glitter
and glossy varnish spray.
Small Christmas baubles
hold individual heads of
Phalaenopsis orchids.

LEFT **Natural sponge**
An accessory with a difference: coiled lengths of sponge complement the green *Anthurium* arranged here on a screen created using a lacing technique.

BELOW **Buttons**
Colour-coordinated buttons form an interesting feature and complement the *Gloriosa* perfectly. Coils of recycled cardboard have been pinned to form an interesting mechanic for the placement of the flowers.

RIGHT **Stones**
Stones at the base of the container provide ballast for stability and also add decorative detail that contrasts with the swirl of the *Schoenus* (flexi grass) and *Xerophyllum tenax* (bear grass).

Candles
An eclectic mix of glass containers grouped and filled with spring flowers, interspersed with candles, provides different forms and additional interest.

Candles
A fresh spring design of
multiple placements
enhanced by the addition
of flickering candles in
votives at different heights.

Candles
Church candles have been placed in elegant brass hurricane-lamp holders, which are ideal for safety and for excluding draughts. They have been positioned at regular intervals along a walkway to enhance the atmosphere created by the flowers.

Elements of design

W hen selecting your flowers and foliage be aware of the use of the elements to ensure that all parts of your design are harmonious.

The elements of design are:

- form
- colour
- texture
- space

RIGHT **Texture**
In this design beautiful textural contrast is evident between the fluffy wool and the smooth *Sandersonia*, *Zantedeschia* (calla) and orchids.

Form

Form can be a mass of flowers of a single variety or a combination of round (such as *Gerbera*), line (such as *Gladiolus*) or spray (such as *Gypsophila*). When the forms are mixed, a round flower is often but not always included to provide focus where the eye can rest.

BELOW LEFT The round forms of *Dianthus barbatus* 'Green Trick', *Dianthus* (carnation), roses and gilded *Papaver* (poppy) seed heads are combined with the spray form of *Trachelium* and the linear *Equisetum* (snake grass).

Colour

Colour schemes can be achromatic (black and white), monochromatic (tints, tones and shades of one colour), adjacent (closely linked), opposite (when the contrasts are dramatic) or polychromatic (different colours).

BELOW In this design an achromatic colour scheme is provided by black sea kelp and white *Anthurium* and *Gypsophila*.

A monochromatic colour scheme based on the colour red, with dark red succulents, red roses, pink mini *Gerbera* and spray *Rosa*, light pink spray *Chrysanthemum* and cherry-pink *Matthiola* (stock).

An adjacent colour scheme using one quarter of the colour wheel is created with colourful bracts of *Physalis alkekengi var.* 'Franchetii' (Chinese lantern) in different stages of maturity and wool pastilles bound on aluminium wire to give contrast of form.

Two vases, one filled with green *Hydrangea* and the other with red roses, offer a design of complementary colours.

A polychromatic design using every colour of the rainbow: yellow, green, orange, red, blue and purple.

Texture

Textural contrasts can be sharp or subtle. When the colours are subdued – for example, when using dried or freeze-dried plant material – there is greater need for contrast.

The block of concrete at the base offers an unconventional textural contrast with the plant material.

Smooth-petalled roses have been combined with rough-textured *Thymus* (thyme) and sharp pebbles for pleasing textural contrasts.

Space

Space is integral to design, as without it there is no form. Space can also be incorporated under, within and around a design.

BELOW In this fine contemporary design the strength of the enclosed space is a key element.

RIGHT Here the space around the placements links the various modules that make up the overall design.

ABOVE AND LEFT This design at the Flowers@Oxford show had visitors spellbound. Multiple strands of wool were criss-crossed over a large iron circle until the construction was strong. Mitsumata branches were then woven through the strands and 1,000 perspex tubes were bound into the structure to hold fragrant Moerman double lilies. Lengths of wool were linked from the structure to the Steinway piano, so that the space created was a major feature of the design.

Principles of design

After using the elements of design to select your flowers and foliage follow the principles of design to ensure it is pleasing to the eye. These principles are:

- balance
- proportion
- scale
- dominance
- contrast
- rhythm

RIGHT Contrast
In this design there are contrasts of light and dark, tall and short, and round and conical forms, with *Freesia* as the constant element.

Balance

Visual and actual balance
should always be evident.

RIGHT An asymmetric
line flows through a
symmetric structure, with
the white *Phalaenopsis*
blooms (top right)
balancing the leaves and
roots (bottom left).

ABOVE Symmetric balance has been achieved
here by the placement of an equal weight of plant
material on each side of an imaginary central line.

This is a good example of how an asymmetrically balanced design should be positioned off-centre. The mass to the left balances the length and space beneath to the right.

Balance
A hollowed-out polystyrene sphere was covered with tape for extra strength and to facilitate the gluing on of pieces of *Pinus* (pine) bark. Foam was inserted into the sphere to support flowers, fruits and berries, including *Clematis* and *Echinacea*. The shape was then placed on a forked branch.

Proportion

Proportion can be used classically, which is when the plant material dominates the container, or it can be reversed so that the container dominates.

A timeless design for spring, where the proportion of flowers to container is 1.5:1.
A modern twist is given by the massing of plant material, with space only around the edges.

ABOVE   Proportion
Here the proportions are reversed, with the ratio of volume of the container to flowers and foliage being about 1.5:1.

RIGHT   Proportion
With limited plant material, proportions often relate to height and width rather than to volume.

Scale

As a general rule, in classic design no flower or leaf is more than twice the size of the one next to it. In contemporary design such considerations of scale do not always hold true, with juxtapositioning knowing no bounds.

RIGHT   Conventionally, the *Anthurium* would seem to be too large in comparison with the *Craspedia*. However, the relative number of *Craspedia* and their dominant colour balance the more subdued green to create the illusion of the *Anthurium* being in scale.

Dominance

This is where, by virtue of colour, form or texture, one part of a design holds the eye and compels attention over the others. Dominance can be subtle or exaggerated.

Massed spray *Chrysanthemum* blooms cover a hollowed-out hemisphere of floral foam. A single red rose dominates through size, colour and central positioning, despite the number of yellow flower heads.

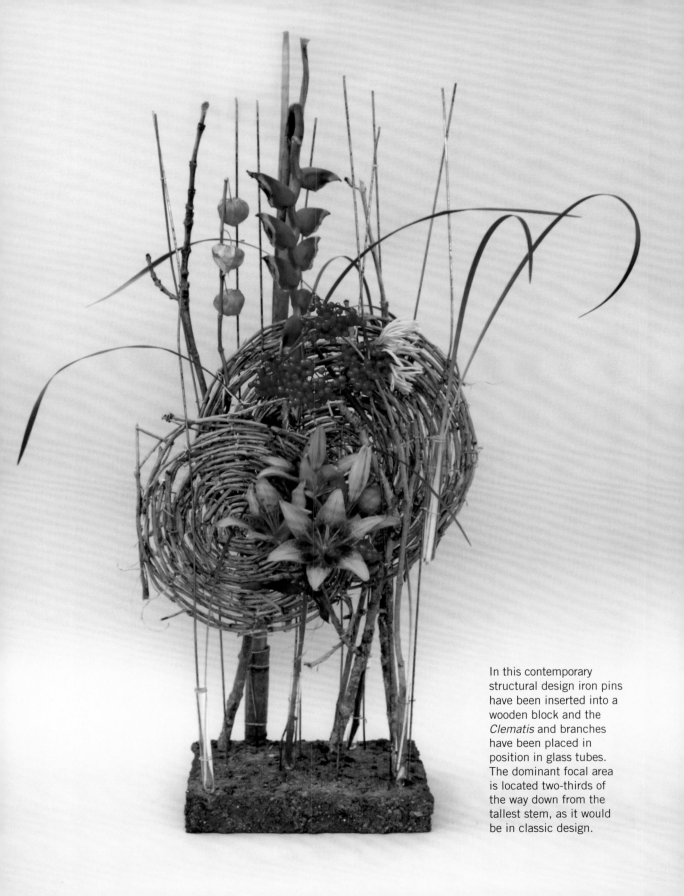

In this contemporary structural design iron pins have been inserted into a wooden block and the *Clematis* and branches have been placed in position in glass tubes. The dominant focal area is located two-thirds of the way down from the tallest stem, as it would be in classic design.

An unconventional use of dominance is shown here with a hanging sphere of *Craspedia* set among an atomic structure of linear foliage and smaller units of flowers. It works thanks to the linkage of form and colour.

Contrast

Contrast avoids monotony and, as with dominance, can be subtle or exaggerated.

Although the bark coils have a greater surface area, the green baubles and candles dominate by virtue of their colour, texture and central placement.

A strong contrast exists
between the circular
and linear movement of
this design.

Contrast
Fluffy white *Gypsophila* is the perfect contrast to the smooth *Anthurium* and the rough-textured black sea kelp.

Rhythm

Rhythm can be created through the repetition of placements, form, colour and texture or through radiation of stems from a central core.

ABOVE AND BELOW Multiple placements give rhythmic movement and hold the eye.

ABOVE Repetition of plant material radiating from the centre creates rhythm.

RIGHT Beautiful rhythm has been created through the use of round flowers on a round form and the circle of trailing *Ceropegia*.

Techniques

E very book and every designer will offer different techniques, and these can include plant, stem and leaf manipulation. Stems and plant fibres that are flexible and colourful and leaves that are tough, strong and long-lasting, such as *Aspidistra*, *Cordyline* (ti), *Cornus* (dogwood), raffia and *Salix* (willow), are the ideal candidates. The list that follows includes the different techniques that I believe have staying power and are easy to use:

- angling/bending
- baling
- binding
- cable tying
- caging
- clamping
- doubling and spearing
- folding and pleating
- framing
- gluing
- grouping
- layering
- looping
- making units
- massing
- pastilles
- piercing
- pinning
- plaiting and scoubidou
- rolling
- stacking
- threading
- veiling
- weaving
- winding

RIGHT **Gluing**
The individual scales of pine cones were removed and glued together to create a mass of interesting texture in a completely different form through manipulation.

Angling/bending

Certain sorts of plant material, notably different grasses, can be bent easily to create eye-catching and intriguing shapes.

Equisetum (snake grass) is easy to manipulate into angular shapes to give interest and structure to a design.

Baling

Compressing hay, straw or other fine material to create geometric shapes.

Cut and compressed raffia has been spray-glued to a circular form, leaving an indentation for the insertion of foam and green and yellow flowers.

Binding

Creating a single unit by taking several elements and tying them together. Among the most common bindings are wool, thread and wire, but plant material itself can also be used.

Cable tying

Cable ties fix components together tightly and securely. They can be used unobtrusively by choosing muted colours and cutting the ends short or in a more flamboyant way by choosing bright colours and leaving the excess as part of the design.

ABOVE Cable tying
An intricate structure of twigs has been held together using trimmed cable ties, with a detail of *Phalaenopsis* orchids.

LEFT Cable tying
Here colourful untrimmed cable ties secure a structure of *Cornus* (dogwood). Roses and *Ranunculus* have been threaded through the structure into mini glass jugs, while mini *Gerbera* at the base give focal interest.

RIGHT Binding
Red and green *Cornus* (dogwood) stems have been bound together with wire to create undulating structures.

Caging

A second open structure around or over a design, often using grasses, reeds, stems or other plant material, to add volume and interest.

RIGHT Units of string were arranged in a criss-cross pattern and sprayed with PVA glue to harden them. They were then fixed together to create a cage for a mass of *Hippeastrum* (amaryllis) on a bed of *Pteridium* (bracken).

A cage of bleached cane encases a low design of *Dianthus barbatus* 'Green Trick', *Eustoma* (lisianthus) and spray roses in a raised dish.

BELOW *Pinus* (pine) needles were threaded through two hemispheres of the same size. *Vanda* 'Tayanee White' orchids were placed in tubes and the two hemispheres were bound together with paper-covered wire (bind wire) and placed on a beautiful Mobach ceramic bowl. Finally *Xerophyllum tenax* (bear grass) was woven through.

RIGHT Stems of *Schoenus* (flexi grass) were inserted into a painted square of insulation board on which a circle had been marked. The free ends of the grass were brought over and fixed down to create a cage for heads of *Vanda* orchid and *Hydrangea*.

Clamping

The use of a device or devices to exert pressure to keep mechanics or plant material in a fixed position.

Rubber bands clamp tubes between wooden blocks to give support for a mix of colourful *Gerbera*, *Freesia* and spray *Dianthus* (carnation).

Magnolia grandiflora leaves have been clamped in place with pegs to provide containers for tubes containing *Cyclamen*, *Rosa*, *Skimmia* flowers and *Vanda* orchids.

Doubling and spearing

A leaf manipulation achieved by doubling a strong, broad strap leaf, such as *Aspidistra* or *Cordyline* (ti), onto itself at a slight angle. The stem end is then brought up and pushed through a central portion of the two layers of leaf.

RIGHT A simple open cage of *Schoenus* (flexi grass) not only adds space but also increases the size of the design of *Phalaenopsis* orchids and manipulated *Aspidistra* leaves which have been doubled and speared.

Dianthus (carnation) create a wonderful mass of colour and texture, while the doubled and speared *Aspidistra* leaves give additional interest.

Folding and pleating

Leaves can be folded and pleated in various ways to neaten their appearance and make them more uniform or to create interesting effects.

Aspidistra leaves have been folded and manipulated here to create a fan-shaped leaf which looks particularly effective when used in such a large-scale design with *Cymbidium* orchids.

Influenced by origami, this design has a traditional Japanese feel. *Aspidistra* leaves were used, with the mid-rib removed so that they could be folded easily.

Framing

The positioning of plant material so that it is bounded or half-enclosed by other, usually organic, material.

LEFT An interesting piece of wood frames six *Lilium* (lily) perfectly.

Gluing

There are many types of glue but all will adhere one dry surface to another (turn to page 415).

BELOW Squares of birch were glued onto circles of strong aluminium wire, which were then spiralled to create dramatic impact through repetition of form and movement.

Gluing
An irregular shape was cut from a piece of polystyrene, then the centre was removed and a trench made for the insertion of foam. Small pieces of *Cobra* leaf were glued to the polystyrene, which was glued to the forked branches and a metal pin was inserted. *Amaranthus*, *Passiflora* (passion flower), *Rosa*, *Viburnum* and apples were added.

Grouping

Grouping and massing are similar, but when plant material is grouped each form keeps its own individual identity rather than becoming part of an indeterminate mass.

The colour, form and texture of the potatoes provide surprise and interest when combined with groups of *Chrysanthemum* 'Santini' and *Papaver* (poppy) seed heads.

Groupimg
n this circular design the stems of *Galax*, roses and fir are grouped to show the individual forms clearly.

Layering

The regular placement of leaves or other plant material on top of each other so that part of the previous placement is visible.

BELOW AND RIGHT Overlapping layered *Galax* leaves create a look that is both repetitive and at the same time distinctive.

Looping

The manipulation of a leaf so that it is curved or doubled over. It can be secured by staples, adhesive or tape.

RIGHT A versatile container that has enclosed spaces is ideal for manipulating *Phormium* leaves into undulating loops and twists by threading the leaves through one space and up into another, thereby creating rhythm, depth and interest.

Looping A mass of looped *Aspidistra* leaves covers three round discs with a feature of white *Anthurium*.

Making units (also known as making modules)

Combining different parts to make a larger whole: the parts can be bound together with paper-covered wire, aluminium, decorative or bullion wire, fabric, cable ties, raffia or glue.

Units made by plaiting 16 lengths of midelino were secured with gold bullion wire terminating in pearl beads. The completed forms were wedged into the network of brown and cream twigs making up the natural container to create a sculptural outline. Green *Cymbidium* heads pick up the colour of the cord on a lichen-decorated sphere inserted behind a group of brown *Bergenia* 'Eroica' leaves.

Units were created from 2 mm galvanised garden wire, brown-paper tape and paper-covered wire (spray-painted) decorated with fragments of dried *Eucalyptus* bark. Further units of brown-paper-covered wire scrunched up with decorative and bullion reel wire were added, producing a zigzag form which was then secured to a metal rod set in a piece of brick. Various fresh *Aeonium* succulents and pea-like *Senecio rowleyanus* run through the design, giving contrast of form, colour, texture and interest.

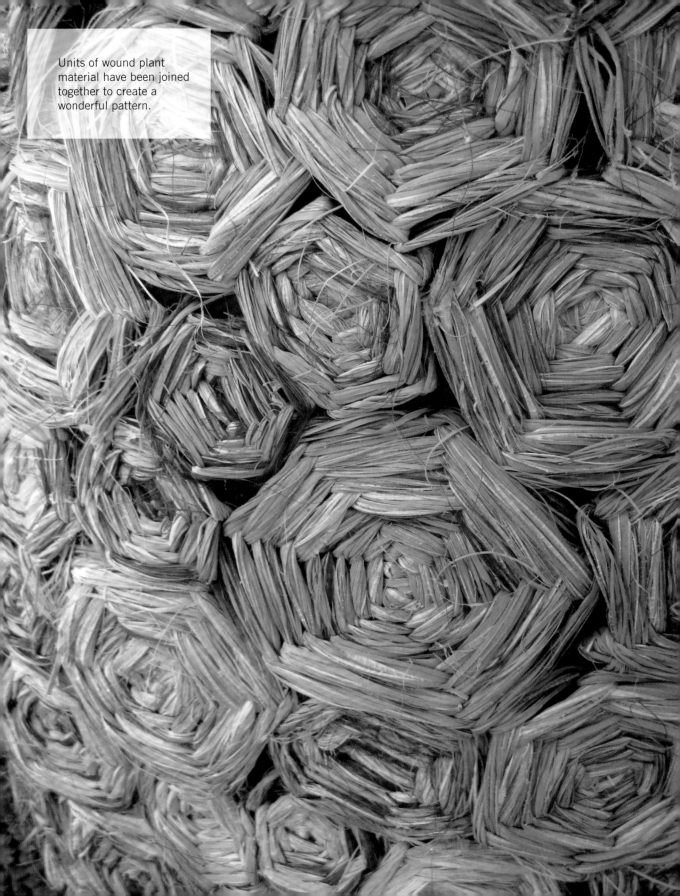

Units of wound plant material have been joined together to create a wonderful pattern.

A 'flower' form hand-tied bouquet was created using units made from 2 mm galvanised garden wire, OASIS® Parchment Wrap and OASIS® Crazy Mesh around a central cluster of wooden golf tees decorated with yellow buttons. *Craspedia* provided interest and a frill of variegated *Aspidistra* neatened the underside. Wired wool cord covered the binding of pot tape.

Making units
A bunch of *Cornus* (dogwood) stems was bound with reel wire, then individual pieces were wired into the bunch and turned at intervals to make a fan-like structure. The two units (fans) were brought together to produce a sculpture.

Massing (also known as blocking, basing or pillowing)

The placing of plant material together so that the whole, rather than the individual forms, stands out.

At the base of the design *Chrysanthemum* have been massed to create strong areas of colour, form and texture. The mini *Gerbera* provide detail.

Pastilles

The wrapping of organic material, such as wool or raffia, around a non-organic filament, such as aluminium wire, to create a trail of varying thicknesses.

LEFT Raffia has been bound around an inner bowl and then wrapped round aluminium wire to create pastilles of varying thickness strong enough to hold stems of *Gloriosa superba* 'Rothschildiana'.

Piercing

The pushing of one kind of organic or inorganic material into or through an object in order to provide support for another kind.

RIGHT Using a 0.3 mm bit, holes were drilled down a column of wood and bamboo cocktail sticks were inserted. Small tubes were covered with sisal, then wedged between the cocktail sticks and filled with *Vanda* orchids. Trailing material was woven down the structure.

Piercing
Sea kelp arches over a low container. Sharp twigs pierce the kelp and give support to glass tubes holding horizontal lines of white *Zantedeschia* (calla) and *Vanda* orchid with *Hypericum* berries and *Passiflora* (passion flower) trails creating decorative interest.

ABOVE AND RIGHT **Piercing**
Oliver Ferchland started by piercing one stem of
Triticum (wheat) with a barbecue stick. He then built
up an intricate structure by repeating the method. This
was sprayed with a solution of wood glue and water to
make it strong. The flowers in his composition were
Daucus, *Leycesteria*, *Ornithogalum* and *Zinnia*.

Pinning

The use of pins or wires to secure one object, which is usually flat, to another.

LEFT Leaves have been manipulated – folded, layered and pinned – to form a column that extends beyond a vase displaying a few perfect pink roses.

RIGHT Different-coloured pins have been used in this creative design. Steel pins and decorative green- and black-headed pins hold *Populus alba* (silver poplar) leaves, sections of *Stachys byzantina* leaves and *Hydrangea* florets in place.

Plaiting and scoubidou

Plaiting is the twisting or braiding together of three or more lengths. Scoubidou is a knotting craft that uses flat or supple hollow threads or tubes in multiples of two.

A braid of *Schoenus* (flexi grass) gives detail and strength to a fan of the same material. The design is finished with a single *Vanda* orchid bloom.

This 'chain' was made from several metres of small, white, flat rattan reed using the scoubidou technique with four strands. It was wound into a circle to create a bouquet holder that was placed in a vase. The container was made by melting white candles and pouring the wax over a glass vase. *Rhododendron* were then placed in small ball vases and decorated with Christmas baubles.

Rolling

The wrapping of regularly spaced leaves around themselves to give new definition.

OASIS® Designer Sheet, lightly dipped in water so it was not too heavy, was used for the top part. A long tray at the base contained foam covered with stabilised *Quercus* (oak) leaves. This was then attached to the back of the designer sheet with mitsumata branches. *Cordyline* (ti) leaves were rolled and stapled together and inserted into the foam in a row. Thick wires were fed into the *Equisetum* (snake grass) stems to create a sturdy structure for the *Phalaenopsis* orchids in tubes covered with *Aspidistra*.

Rolling
An Oasis® Designer Sheet was covered with *Anthurium* leaves. Additional *Anthurium* were rolled and secured with wire. Several branches created an armature to hold the foam sheet. Long *Vanda* orchid roots were attached to the branch at the top and became the structure to which purple *Vanda*, in *Aspidistra*-covered tubes, were attached.

Stacking

The creation of orderly piles of plant material, usually in layers.

The container was filled with clay and welding rods were inserted at regular intervals. The *Ilex* (holly) leaves and berries were then threaded on the rods to create a stack.

Stacking
A stack of dried
Araucaria (monkey
puzzle) leaves has
been arranged around
a column of foam with
a cheerful topping of
hips and *Dahlia*.

Threading

The placing of organic or inorganic
material on a slender, flexible filament to
create a continuous line.

Small succulents and
pearls have been
threaded on wire to give
decorative detail and help
keep the leaves in place.

Veiling

The placement of light or delicate plant material over a more compact form to partly conceal it and to provide interest, contrast and an extra dimension.

RIGHT This hand-tied with a woven collar has a veiled covering of *Shoenus* (flexi grass).

BELOW *Pandanus* (fountain grass), *Liriope* (lily grass) and trails of *Diplocyclos* veil a compact structure of hollow stems holding *Gerbera*, *Gloriosa* and *Craspedia*.

Weaving

The joining together of two materials, organic or inorganic, to create patterns.

RIGHT Ribbon has been woven through an *Aspidistra* leaf to give colour and interest.

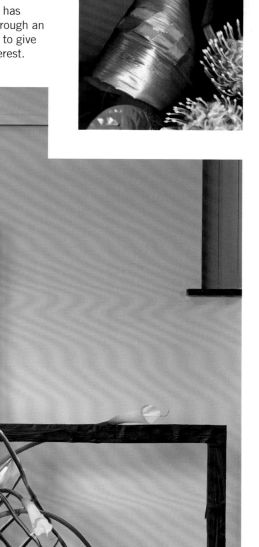

LEFT Strands of *Xerophyllum tenax* (bear grass), with the flat side uppermost, were woven uniformly through copper mesh to create movement. The design was finished by adding a thin wire around the edge to keep the grass within the frame and then decorated with white *Dendrobium* (Singapore orchid).

ABOVE A wire was placed between two *Dianella ensifolia* (umbrella dracaena) leaves and they were joined with double-sided tape so that wavy movements could be created. They were then attached to a wooden frame held together with metal clasps.

Winding

Multiple turns of a
soft material to create
a continuous coil.

Skeins of raffia were
wound and mounted to
create vertical interest.

LEFT Winding
Aspidistra sections were wound and coiled, then interspersed with moss attached to a sphere. Three white *Gloriosa* provided a special touch.

RIGHT Decorative fibre bound on wire creates a swirl of interest around the vertical stems of *Delphinium*.

BELOW Winding
Sinuous coils of *Schoenus* (flexi grass) were wound round three spheres with connecting highlights of white *Anthurium*.

Original
containers

For something a bit different, containers can be created from all sorts of natural and inorganic materials. There is no limit to what can be used, but the most dramatic containers tend to be made from one sort of material at a time. You could experiment with any of the following:

- acorn cups
- bark
- bindwire
- card and paper
- cones
- flattened cane
- husks
- leaves – fresh, dried and preserved
- seed pods
- sticks, stems and branches
- veneer
- wood slices

RIGHT Leaves
The edges of a styrofoam hemisphere were removed with a sharp knife and strips of dried *Pandanus* were hot-glued to the shape so they abutted. Tubes containing *Zinnia* were then placed within the form.

Husks
An S shape was made from chicken wire, reinforced with tape, onto which ears of *Triticum* (wheat) were hot-glued. The structure was then placed on a spike with a heavy base. An indentation was made on one side of the form into which foam was placed so that *Amaranthus*, *Anemone*, *Dahlia*, roses and sycamore seeds could be added.

Branches
Branches of birch were
fixed together with a
staple gun. Bleached
Jatropha podagrica
(Buddha belly plant)
seed pods were attached
using the same method
to provide containers
for small orchid plants
and moss.

RIGHT **Leaves**
Typha grass has been
manipulated around a
metal stand to create a
fresh green container for
a mass of mini *Gerbera*
and *Dianthus* (carnation).

Reeds
A plastic container was
covered with double-
sided tape to which
Equisetum (snake grass)
was adhered. *Anthurium*
and *Liriope* (lily grass)
completed the design.

Seed pods
Horizontal lines of black *Zantedeschia* (calla) are threaded through bare twigs that hold exotic seed pods with *Phalaenopsis* orchid blooms, all arranged over a tray of *Gomphocarpus physocarpus* fruits.

RIGHT Leaves
Dried lotus leaves have been placed all round an inexpensive container, then secured and decorated with garlands of threaded succulent leaves and pearls.

LEFT Flattened cane
A shape was cut from a polystyrene sphere and then extended with wire and tape. Pieces of white wood were glued over the resulting container, which holds *Amaranthus*, *Eustoma* (lisianthus), *Dianthus barbatus* 'Green Trick', *Rosa* and *Vanda* orchid roots. *Panicum* (fountain grass) has been sprayed with glue and brought over towards the middle of the design.

RIGHT Bindwire
This decorative container was created using coiled and twisted paper-covered wire (bindwire).

ABOVE **Veneer**
The form of a wine carafe was extended with chicken wire
bound with tape. This was then covered with bleached
veneer and filled with David Austin roses and grasses.

Stems
Short lengths of *Cornus* (dogwood) were used to decorate the rim of a handmade bowl covered with pieces of veneer.

BELOW Stems
Dried flower stems were used to create a wheel-like structure through and against which flowers have been positioned.

RIGHT Seedheads
A lovely textural design for a summer's day made from a hemisphere of polystyrene to which *Cotinus coggygria* (smoke tree) fluff has been spray-glued in layers (several layers were necessary). The plant material includes *Cosmos* 'Black Beauty', *Phalaenopsis* orchids, *Viburnum opulus* berries, *Scabiosa* fruits and *Thymus* (thyme).

ABOVE Card and paper

Moniek Vanden Berghe has used corrugated paper and
card to great effect in creating these containers, giving
them interesting and contrasting textures. The cone
contains a glass full of foliage, while the bowl of flowers
sits balanced on top like a scoop of ice cream.

RIGHT AND FOLLOWING PAGES Stems

Short lengths of *Heracleum* (hogweed) were bound
together with OASIS® Bindwire to create a round
structure and the outer ring was glued in place.
The central area has been left open for the insertion
of single bloom flowers with their foliage removed.
Warning: *Heracleum* (hogweed) should be handled with
care as it is poisonous and a skin irritant.

LEFT Bark
The three containers were created from polystyrene covered with tape, to which pieces of *Pinus* (pine) bark were glued. These were then filled with berries, grasses and seasonal summer flowers.

RIGHT Sticks
An intricate collection of mikado sticks were glued together to form a boat-shaped container for *Rubus* (blackberry) and *Chelone* (pink turtlehead).

Cones
These natural containers
were made from pine
and other cones.

Bark
A polystyrene shape was covered with tape and *Prunus* bark. The flowers are a mix of *Hydrangea*, *Hypericum*, *Nerine*, *Pieris*, *Rosa* 'Coral Luna' and *Skimmia*.

Structures

A structure is a decorative support for mechanics and/or plant material that is created from fresh or dried organic material. It can be created from inorganic material covered with natural plant material. Structures can be secured with wire, cable ties, nails, paper-covered wire (bindwire), common raffia or even pegs or paperclips. Some of the principal materials used to create a structure are:

- twigs, stems, branches
- cane
- grasses and reeds

Note: I have used the term 'constructions' for supports made from inorganic material that are **not** covered with organic material.

RIGHT Short lengths of *Betula* (birch) were bound together with paper-covered wire (bindwire) to create an interesting structure of twigs. Glass tubes holding *Zantedeschia* (calla) and *Galax* leaves were then attached.

LEFT *Brassica napus* (rape seed) stems have been inverted so the roots are uppermost to provide a structure to support the fresh flower stems.

RIGHT A cane structure supports arching stems of *Phalaenopsis* orchids and woven strands of *Liriope* (lily grass).

ABOVE Stems have been bound together with wire to create structural units. Further stems were cut short and wired over a moss ball.

LEFT A simple structure of lichen-covered branches was created to support the smooth stems of *Allium, Nerine, Rosa, Trachelium* and *Zantedeschia* (calla).

RIGHT Long grasses have been meticulously bound into huge metal supports. The inner frame is filled with a mass of *Dianthus* (carnation).

A horizontal structure straddles a lily vase with multiple hanging *Physalis alkekengi var.* 'Franchetii' (Chinese lantern), *Zantedeschia* (calla) and some festive baubles.

Cornus (dogwood) can create a large, long-lasting contemporary structure without huge cost. This stunning star shape needed only the designer's inspiration and a lot of patience!

The fantastic curving
rhythm of this cane
structure gives
uplifting movement.

Styles

Using the flowers and foliage, the mechanics, the accessories and the techniques already described, designers have come up with a range of contemporary styles, including:

- collage
- floral fashions and jewels
- floral pictures
- flowers in a vase
- hand-tieds
- hanging designs
- in, on or between the container
- jam jars, bottles and glasses
- long-lasting, freeze-dried, preserved and waxed flowers and foliage
- montage
- multiple placements
- palisades/fencing
- parallel design
- screens
- spheres
- tapestries, cushions and floral cakes
- transparencies
- waterfalls
- wedding bouquets

RIGHT Wedding bouquet
This innovative bridal bouquet by Lana Bates featured lily petals assembled to create the composite centrepiece. The surround was made using two carton discs covered with lengths of gypsum bandage and decorated with patterns of glue. Fur was added to complete this stunning design.

Collage

A collage is a two-dimensional textured work on a flat backing. Some of the most effective collages are designs using petals.

Go with your heart: a collage of petals on white canvas using *Gerbera* for the heart, mini *Gerbera* for the boat and paper for the sea. The mast was created from the stem of a star fern using Mod Podge and floral adhesive.

A swirl of *Gerbera* petals with *Dianthus barbatus* (sweet william) and *Alstroemeria*. The centre is composed of the silver spear-like *Astelia* leaves.

Floral fashions and jewels

From elaborate dresses to simple jewellery, long-lasting foliage and flowers are being used as personal decoration.

BELOW   A bridal circlet of *Hydrangea*.

RIGHT   This dress of *Vanda* orchids with *Stachys byzantina* detail was created for the sponsors of Chelsea Flower Show. The model had to walk a long way wearing the dress, so the technique was more complex than it would have been for a static model. The dress was built on a fabric bodice and *Vanda* was chosen for its relatively flat form, plus its ability to survive out of water. It lasted a week.

LEFT The train of this stunning dress was constructed, from the waist down, using chicken wire on a model. A pattern was created using stiff brown paper to which *Cocos nucifera* (coconut) leaves were hot-glued, following lines drawn on the paper. This was placed over the chicken-wire shape. The hair was also created from chicken wire, which was covered with *Ficus* leaves. Glass tubes were inserted into the hair shape and filled with *Gloriosa*. *Dianthus* (carnation) were then added to the pattern on the dress, inserted into the chicken wire through cuts in the paper. *Gomphrena* were glued on and the dress was finished with cut *Pandanus* leaves. The bolero top was made separately using the same technique.

RIGHT Light, textural *Heracleum* (hogweed) stems with their intricate dried structure formed the base of this floral headpiece. A dense cluster of *Cymbidium* 'Ice Cascade', *Cyclamen persicum*, *Paphiopedilum* (slipper orchid) and *Eucharis* (Amazon lily) were glued to the base, with lighter, more spaced placements towards the periphery.

LEFT This decorated bag was created from chicken wire covered with tape, to which lengths of interesting wired wool and threads were glued. Foam was placed in a hollow in the top and filled with a mix of roses and some lengths of *Hoya linearis*.

RIGHT Petals, leaves, succulents and tiny flower heads have been layered and woven onto this mask and necklace to create a jewel-encrusted floral effect.

Floral pictures

Three-dimensional works within boundaries which become an effective picture.

A floral picture created on a narrow ledge fitted with a wooden façade and base (held in place with lead weights) which effectively hide the mechanics for the *Fatsia* leaves and white *Anthurium*. A branch of *Sambucus* (elder) was positioned and decorated with dried *Heuchera* leaves and foam spheres covered with *Xerophyllum tenax* (bear grass). Short pieces of *Xerophyllum* were inserted into the spheres by bending them at each end to achieve a woven effect and the whole was varnished to make it weatherproof.

RIGHT A floral picture with massed cinnamon slices,
dried *Musa* (banana) inflorescence stalks and
bleached mulberry, with fresh *Zantedeschia* (calla)
and trails of *Ceropegia*.

Flowers in a vase

Contemporary flowers in a vase could be simple designs in a single container or multiple arrangements along a table, placed inside the opening of a container or even angled over the rim.

LEFT A single bloom of *Cymbidium* orchid accompanied by a gilded fir cone and a rolled *Aspidistra* leaf.

RIGHT The pointed ends of a number of conical glass containers have been inserted in floral foam for stability. *Cordyline* (ti) leaves cover the edges of the base, which is filled with *Phlox*, roses and *Viburnum opulus* 'Roseum'. *Nerine* have been placed in the glass cones.

BELOW Multiple placements with tints and shades of purple and red in both flowers and mirror cubes.

BELOW A bronze wire-mesh sheet supports glass 'light-bulb' containers holding double lilies and *Anethum graveolens* (dill). The net is weighed down by the sheer weight of water in the bulbs to create stability.

RIGHT Four containers with the same form and height are the inspiration for an assortment of late spring flowers – *Allium*, *Fritillaria persica* (Persian fritillary), *Hyacinthus* and *Tulipa*.

BELOW Beautiful turquoise-blue containers among clear glass ones of a similar shape allow for an eclectic mix of flowers and foliage, offering charm and panache.

RIGHT In this impressive design, multiple lily vases filled with *Vanda* orchids and hanging *Heliconia* contain coloured water, giving rhythm through repetition of colour. Other flowers include *Guzmania* and *Aechmea* 'Blue Rain'.

Hand-tieds

A hand-tied is a unique, personalised bouquet made with beautiful flowers and foliage with spiralled or parallel stems.

A scented hand-tied of *Hydrangea*, *Matthiola* (stock), *Syringa* (lilac), *Rosa* 'Sweet Avalanche' and *R.* 'Menta', *Viburnum opulus* 'Roseum', blossom and flowering *Eucalyptus*, bound with vintage lace.

In this relaxed and innovative hand-tied of mixed flowers, the rhythm is provided by the magical flow of stripped olive stems from a central core.

A hand-tied with *Centaurea* (cornflower), *Lilium* (lily), *Eucalyptus* and *Rumex* (sorrel) picked from where it was made.

ABOVE An aluminium wire construction formed the basis for this immaculate hand-tied. It was then covered with red *Dianthus* (carnation) and roses, with detail and interest provided by spray *Dianthus*, *Gloriosa*, *Hypericum* berries and *Limonium*.

RIGHT This stylish hand-tied by Per Benjamin uses his trademark colours. Aluminium wire creates circle upon circle of flowers with stems pinned in as part of the design.

LEFT A hand-tied of *Gerbera*, *Hydrangea*, *Rosa* and *Panicum virgatum* (fountain grass), with a collar created from stub wire and shredded raffia.

ABOVE A beautiful vintage hand-tied of roses and *Hydrangea*, with folded and pleated dried lotus leaves, in a container that is in total harmony.

BELOW A hand-tied of *Lilium* (lily) with a decorative, woven *Typha* leaf column around the stems.

Hanging designs

These provide a wealth of opportunities for decorating walls, windows and open spaces.

LEFT Thick stems of *Bambusa* (bamboo) were sliced into small sections, bent into circles and bound with cable ties. They were then attached to a ceiling light fixture, one by one, to create the structure. Small glass tubes were added and filled with water before white *Anthurium*, cut short, were inserted.

RIGHT Suspended metal circles have been bound with wool of different widths and textures and embellished with *Anthurium*, *Dianthus* (carnation) and *Gloriosa superba* 'Rothschildiana'.

Raffia-covered circles hold countless trails made from small sections of cut stems joined with bind wire. Individual heads of the glorious *Clematis* have been placed in glass tubes at strategic points. This is a work for the enthusiast!

Gilded skeletonised leaves and glass ornaments have been combined to create an effective window hanging. The look is completed at the base with structures of *Pinus* (pine) needles holding mini vases containing *Eucharis* (Amazon lily).

This exquisite hanging disc uses individual heads of *Phalaenopsis* orchids and delicate *Ginkgo* leaves on perspex. Trails of *Ceropegia* add rhythm.

Beaded hangings support glass tubes holding *Syringa* (lilac) and lime-green *Eustoma* (lisianthus). *Tillandsia usneoides* (Spanish moss) gives textural contrast, while festive ornaments complete the picture.

Hanging

Red and orange spray roses and *Viburnum* berries form
the base of this luxurious wreath on a foam frame. The
wintry *Senecio cineraria* contrasts well against the warm
colours. *Humulus lupulus* (hop) trails finish the design.

In, on or between the container

This new way of looking at design, which seems to defy nature, can rely on super-balance, the repetition of multiple placements or the use of long-lasting plant material that can survive happily either under or out of water.

Tulipa and *Zantedeschia* (calla) stems rest on the rim of the containers with their ends in crystal-clear water, while *Anemone* and *Tulipa* blooms give visual weight at the base.

LEFT Foam at the top of the vase allows *Gypsophila* to hang down inside, while *Phalaenopsis* orchids, *Aspidistra* and baubles decorate the top.

RIGHT The top of a tall glass container holds a low container with foam for the arrangement of a mass of wonderful spring flowers. *Syringa* (lilac), *Eustoma* (lisianthus), *Viburnum opulus* 'Roseum' and cherry blossom are included in this exuberant design.

A second bowl was placed inside the first and glued in position. Water was added between the two and a gorgeous display of seasonal flowers – *Lathyrus* (sweet pea), *Achillea* and *Dianthus* (carnation) – slotted into position.

Jam jars, bottles and glasses

Seemingly casual, unstructured placements of flowers in simple glass containers are very much in vogue. They create their effect through multiplication and a common theme.

ABOVE These unsophisticated arrangements in a sophisticated setting work through the grouping of simple flowers in pastel tints.

BELOW Jam jars holding *Hydrangea*, *Matthiola* (stock), *Syringa* (lilac), *Rosa* 'Sweet Avalanche' and *R.* 'Menta', *Viburnum opulus* 'Roseum', blossom and flowering *Eucalyptus*.

A multitude of simple textured glass containers contain *Astrantia*, *Rosa* 'Avalanche' and *Syringa* (lilac).

Long-lasting, freeze-dried, preserved and waxed flowers and foliage

Freeze-dried flowers are subtly coloured and relatively fragile, as moisture has been extracted from the petals. Moisture has also been removed from flowers that have been preserved, but it has been replaced by natural chemicals and glycerine, so they are more robust. However, as preserved flowers turn brown, they need to be dipped in dye of various hues to look fresh rather than dead! Both freeze-dried and preserved flowers have extremely short stems and designs need to be created bearing this in mind. Preserved foliage is easy to use but can be expensive. 'Waxed flowers' have been created by dipping tissue into hot wax.

BELOW Freeze-dried *Helleborus* and *Dianthus* (carnation) with *Populus alba* (silver poplar) leaves retain their form perfectly with muted colours.

RIGHT Beautiful freeze-dried Agora roses and *Delphinium*.

BELOW A structured mass of preserved roses on a bed of *Hydrangea* in a subtle palette of colours.

RIGHT Garlands are often inaccessible and need long-lasting plant material, especially things that survive out of water. In this design *Amaranthus*, *Chrysanthemum*, *Physalis alkekengi var.* 'Franchetii' (Chinese lantern), *Malus* (crab apple) and *Vanda* orchid heads work perfectly.

LEFT Freeze-dried
A structure of threaded *Populus alba* (silver poplar) leaves, a few heads of *Helleborus* and green *Hydrangea.*
As the stems of freeze-dried flowers are short or non-existent, this design is ideal.

RIGHT Long-lasting
All members of the Proteaceae family last well even out of water. Here *Protea magnifica* (queen protea) have been inserted into glass tubes through flat cane, together with *Ilex verticillata* (deciduous holly).

Waxed 'flowers' were created by dipping pieces of tissue into hot wax and wrapping them round heavy-gauge wires to form a flower-like shape. After they had dried all the waxed 'flowers' were inserted into scaffolding board to create a base that looked light and fluffy. All along the board additional wires were added, with glass tubes attached holding fresh *Eustoma* (lisianthus), roses and *Dianthus* (carnation) with leaves placed between. The base of the altar was a thick layer of moss sandwiched between chicken wire and filled with rose hips to give a carpet effect.

Montage

Always three-dimensional, a montage is created by combining different interconnecting layers in an interesting and unusual way. Space between and within the layers plays an important part.

BELOW A naturalistic montage using stones to support spaced layers of slate. Dry seaweed, *Mahonia* berries and curving *Aspidistra* leaves give rhythmic movement throughout and add further layers. *Echeveria*, thrift and dried *Agapanthus* heads are tucked into spaces, providing textural variation.

ABOVE Units were made from assorted green fabric and sisal wound with decorative wire onto lengths of 2 mm galvanised garden wire. These were then attached to a perspex sheet bound with thick black wool and to themselves with cable ties to create interconnecting layers. Distinct areas of space exist under and within the low structure. Moss spheres, purple felt, twisted green aluminium wire and round tiles of black painted and textured lining material add interest. Dark blue-purple *Vanda* and green *Cymbidium* blooms inject fresh colour that harmonises with the other components selected.

RIGHT Bold coloured squares and rectangles are the starting point for this vibrant montage using *Vanda* 'Raspberry Cerise', 'Mokara' orchids, *Chrysanthemum* 'Kermit', *Diplocyclos palmatus*, *Hypericum* 'Coco Yoko' and *Senecio rowleyanus*.

Multiple placements

To create a successful design in a number of containers you need a common theme or feel, such as a shared colour scheme or similar types of containers or of plant material. Multiple placements look good along a table or in a circle, perhaps on a base of mirror glass, slate or wood.

ABOVE The containers may be different shapes and sizes and the flowers may be different colours but continuity is provided by the common theme of glass and roses.

Twin vases are linked through the repetition of colour, form and texture. Trails of *Passiflora* (passion flower) flow between them.

Multiple placements flow along the length of a wedding table to create decoration that can be seen from above, through or around. Just as it should be!

This continuous bank of flowers has been created by using interconnecting placements.

Palisades/fencing

Usually created from series of short lengths of
sticks or branches bound together tightly at
regular intervals, palisades surround a design to
give interest and/or disguise mechanics.

A palisade of *Pinus* (pine) needles was created around a polystyrene base wrapped in double-sided tape. *Ranunculus* and berries were inserted in the hollow in the polystyrene, which had been filled with foam.

A pinned palisade of twigs covers a foam ring, with a polystyrene base that has been halved and repositioned to create an S shape. Within is a low placement of *Eustoma* (lisianthus), roses and *Nerine*.

Parallel design

When parallel design first became popular it had certain characteristics that were strictly adhered to, such as massed plant material, bound stems and no radiation. A looser style has evolved, but although minor radiation is frequently evident the emphasis remains on the vertical. Parallel designs can be either rectangular or circular. Parallel seems a better description than the alternative, landscape, as the style often produces designs that are taller than they are wide.

LEFT *Cornus* (dogwood) stems create vertical movement supported by *Phalaenopsis* orchids, which are repeated at the base with swirls of *Cornus* and trails of *Diplocyclos*.

RIGHT In this parallel design *Stachys byzantina* leaves have been threaded onto vertical rods in a circular fashion, with extra interest provided by individual orchid heads.

FAR RIGHT A circular parallel design with purple *Zantedeschia* 'Paco' (calla), *Anemone* and electric-blue mitsumata sticks bound with coils of purple wool. Purple *Trachelium* 'Lake Michigan' covers the rim of the container, which is decorated with *Vanda* 'Purple Mulberry'.

A parallel design created by impaling heavy-gauge stub wires in a block of wood and attaching glass tubes with cable ties. *Gloriosa* and *Panicum* (fountain grass) provide colour and interest, together with coiled corrugated cardboard at the base and novel placements of *Craspedia*.

Screens

Screens are usually, but not always, floor-standing frames of ironwork, wire or wood with a transparent structure linking the frame embellished with plant material.

This screen was made by criss-crossing wool over a circular metal frame, creating depth in both colour and texture. Here Per Benjamin uses the space under the design to add to the overall impact.

BELOW A screen design created on a narrow metal frame with *Helleborus* threaded through a structure of lime-green wired cord circles. Delicate strands of *Holboellia coriacea* vine run rhythmically throughout. The space to the right is balanced by the mass on the left.

RIGHT Paper-covered wire was criss-crossed over a lacquered iron frame. Inflated balloons were part-wrapped in tape and covered with Paverpol textile hardener, which was allowed to dry. The balloons were then deflated and removed. Plastic film was placed inside the resulting containers, which were then filled with moss, mini orchid plants and trails of *Vanda* roots.

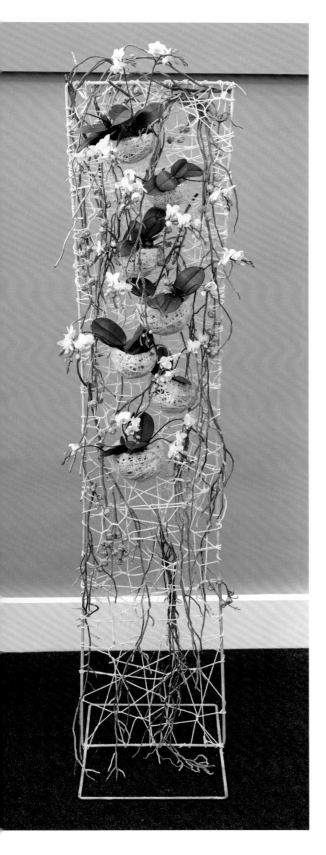

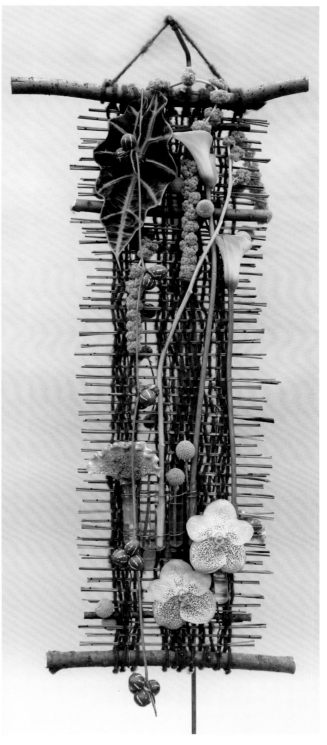

ABOVE This ingenious hanging screen was made from short branches and reeds to which tubes holding *Amaranthus*, *Celosia*, *Craspedia*, *Vanda* orchids, *Zantedeschia* (calla) and an *Alocasia* leaf were attached.

Spheres

Spherical forms can be created from flexible whippy stems such as *Akebia*, *Lonicera* (honeysuckle), *Salix* (willow), *Vitis* (vine) or even thorny *Pyracantha*. They can also have as their base a foam or polystyrene sphere.

BELOW *Pyracantha* stems, stripped of their leaves, have been manipulated into spheres to give support to the *Astrantia major* and *Anthurium*.

RIGHT More than 5,000 stunning multicoloured roses were used to cover the spheres and columns that decorate this banqueting table.

These beautifully colour-coordinated spheres were made by covering foam with wool and ribbon.

LEFT Floral spheres take more flowers than most people imagine, but when they are used in different sizes to complement taller designs the effect is magical.

Tapestries, cushions and floral cakes

A tapestry is a design of small-scale flowers, succulents, interesting natural plant material and inorganic accessories woven together.

A cushion, by comparison, has more rounded sides, appears to be stuffed and generally has a more limited range of plant material.

Floral cakes are often built on a circular foam form with decorated sides and a textured surface. Smaller versions can be made from cupcake holders designed for the cake industry or foam-filled holders produced by SMITHERS-OASIS.

BELOW A star-shaped tapestry with an interesting palisade of cut *Cornus* (dogwood) stems at the base.

ABOVE A cushion of *Pinus* (pine) needles, with detail provided by *Ilex verticillata* (deciduous holly) berries.

LEFT A cushion covered in preserved *Stachys byzantina* leaves with a feature of *Vanda* 'Kanchana® Magic Blue'.

BELOW A floral cake bound with *Aspidistra* and sisal string, filled with *Anemone*, *Tulipa* and *Viburnum tinus*.

A few flower stems in the foam-filled teacup and cupcake holder were all that was needed to create these designs.

BELOW A floral cake with a surround of *Equisetum* (snake grass) topped with short sprigs of fir, rose hips and *Tillandsia* (air plant).

A floral cake covered with the heads of *Chrysanthemum* 'Santini' bearing a single stem of pink *Phalaenopsis* orchid.

Transparencies

In transparencies the fact that light is allowed through a substantial part of the design is integral to the overall effect.

Coiled and twisted gold aluminium wire covers two-thirds of a metal circle, with individual *Phalaenopsis* blooms occupying the remaining third. The overwhelming feeling is one of space and light.

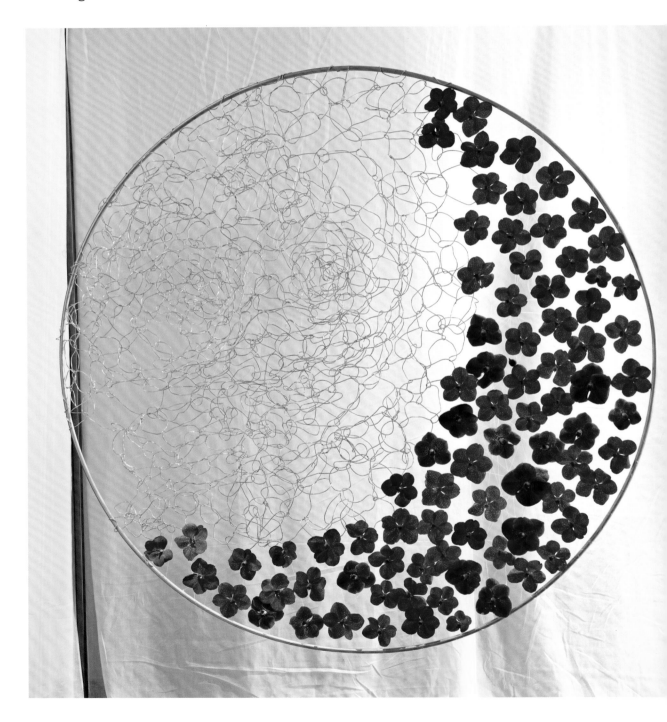

A transparent design of vertically placed *Agapanthus*, *Amaranthus*, *Angelica gigas*, *Campanula*, *Chrysanthemum* and *Iris* with most of the foliage removed. The container, made of soil and wood glue, forms a striking contrast to the flowers.

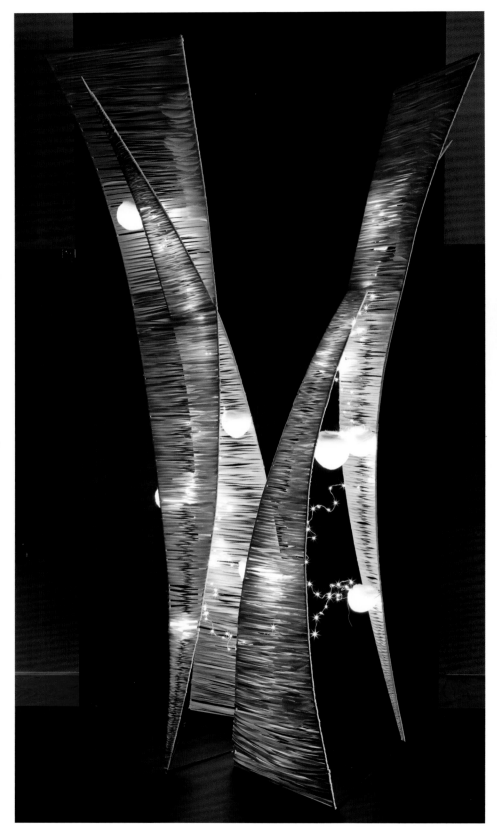

ABOVE AND LEFT
Transparencies
Wax spheres are an interesting feature in this design. The lights glowing through the balls show off their translucency.

Waterfalls

This style of floral design is usually viewed from one side. In order to appreciate the downward flow, it needs to be raised.

A waterfall of *Vanda* orchids and trailing plant material flows from one side of a symmetrically balanced swirl of twigs.

Waterfall
The basic structure was created from chicken wire. This was then covered with plastic tape and supported on a metal spike with a heavy base. A hollow was made for the insertion of foam and flowers. Slices of dried mushrooms were hot-glued onto the structure and *Clematis*, *Gloriosa*, *Leycesteria* and *Rosa* were trailed down.

Wedding bouquets

The form of the wedding bouquet knows no bounds, but ultimately the criteria are that the design is well balanced, light to handle and does not overpower the bride. Collars around the bouquet and embellishments of beads, decorative wire and feathers are all there to be enjoyed if requested.

The glamellia or carmen rose is made from the petals of 12–15 roses surrounding one beautiful bloom. They can be glued or pinned. *Dahlia* and *Lilium* (lily) can also be used to create similar composite flowers, which are exquisite as wedding bouquets.

ABOVE A decorative piece that could easily be adapted to a wedding bouquet with *Vanda* orchids, *Echinops* and spray *Rosa* 'Mini Eden' tumbling through a round gilded frame.

RIGHT A bouquet for autumn showing the wonderful colours of *Gloriosa* and *Grevillea* with dried, coloured grasses.

LEFT A buttonhole using vintage flowers, a perfect partner for a bride wanting muted colours in her bouquet.

ABOVE Lengths of black aluminium wire were manipulated into wavy loops through which beaded wire decorated with *Dendrobium* (Singapore orchid) was threaded.

RIGHT For the bride who loves vintage, a beautiful wedding bouquet of *Rosa* 'Sweet Avalanche', *R.* 'Menta' and *Syringa* 'Maiden's Blush' (lilac) on a base of flowering *Eucalyptus*. The stems of this bouquet were wrapped in lengths of lace.

Land art, installations and natural sculpture

S ometimes it can be quite difficult to differentiate between these three related but distinct concepts.

Land art is usually situated outdoors, perhaps on a beach, up a mountain or in a forest, and consists of manipulated and organised plant material that has been picked up in or derives from a particular location. Land artists sometimes aim to shock and excite by placing objects primarily from natural sources in positions that are at total variance with what might normally be expected.

An installation is a bold, three-dimensional, large-scale work within a limited space that can be situated indoors or outdoors. The frame can be organic or inorganic.

Natural sculpture is often but not always situated in an open expanse of countryside using limited plant material. It can be free-standing or on a man-made frame. It needs to be able to withstand the elements and to last for a significant length of time. It can be as simple as a single found piece of plant material (usually wood) that has been enhanced by cleaning, polishing or even varnishing.

RIGHT **Land art**
A vast expanse of flat land is the setting for billowing sails of palm spathes, one of which is seen here. Horticulturally, this plant material has no connection to where it has been situated, but its placement, with seaweed and driftwood, fits aesthetically with this seascape.

Installation
This large-scale, three-dimensional installation uses the inside of a building in a wide-open space.

ABOVE Installation
The space around this installation is limited by the boundaries of the clipped yew hedge. A natural structure has been created on a man-made frame, with additional interest provided by the use of exotic orchids.

RIGHT Installation
An installation of *Salix babylonica* var. *pekinensis* 'Tortuosa'. (twisted willow) on a bed of different mosses, with decorative detail provided by *Amaranthus*, *Craspedia*, *Crocosmia*, *Hedera helix* (ivy), *Leucospermum* and *Rudbeckia*.

Installation
Disparate components can create an installation when set in close proximity. The red chairs in this design have been placed on a bright green lawn, creating a startling effect through the use of complementary colours. There is a strong suggestion of Surrealism here and the work of the Belgian artist René Magritte.

ABOVE Installation
An indoor installation of *Dahlia* and *Chrysanthemum*. Conical shapes made from bleached palm leaves 'float' on raised glass containers.

RIGHT Sculpture
David Nash, *Two Sliced Cedars*, 2010 (Kew Gardens)
Man and nature come together in Nash's sculpture. Here he took wood from the landscape, charred it and returned it to the landscape. These two monoliths have clearly been tooled into shape by human hand. The blackening of the wood relates to the natural cycle of trees, which eventually turn to coal.

Sculpture
David Nash, *Cork Dome*,
2012 (Kew Gardens)
This sculpture was
inspired by a trip Nash
made to Portugal, where
he stayed on a cork farm.
He relates cork bark to
the human 'outer skin'.

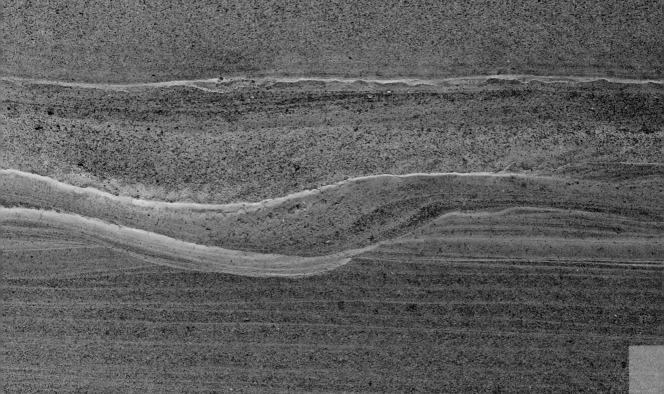

Some of the best

For this book I have chosen the best from the most inspirational designers. But I do have a few special favourites, created by designers whose talent is supreme and who never fail to excite through their mastery of floral design. Here they are.

Contemporary elegance
featuring cane rings by
Stef Adriaenssens.

An installation by
Stef Adriaenssens
that takes
contemporary design
to a new level.

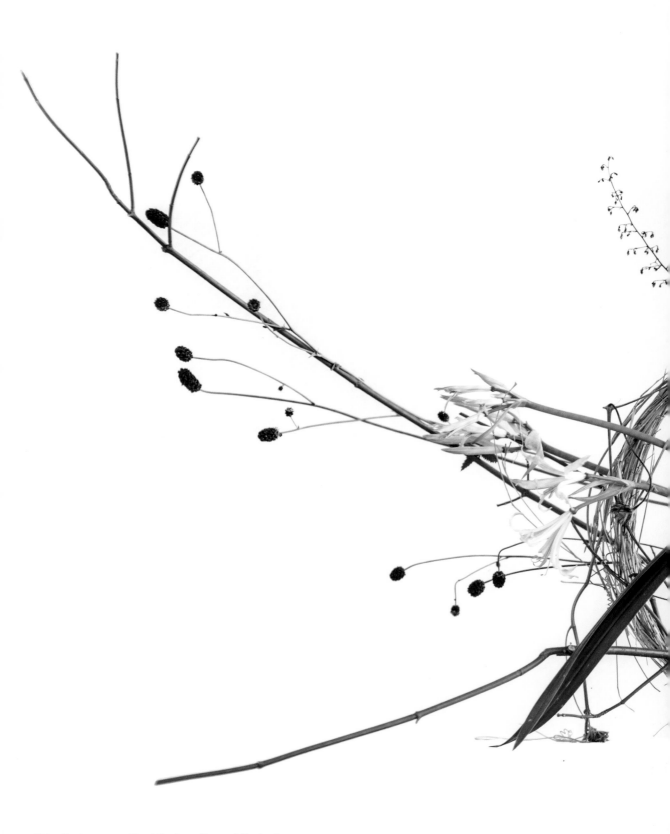

Work by Gregor Lersch in which structure and technique blend seamlessly with design.

Rudy Casati's open book inspires utter amazement at
the technique and joy at the sheer beauty of the design.

An installation of rings and spheres covered in *Hydrangea* by Robin Van Nuffelen.

Six in a row: each container is wrapped in wool of a different texture and colour. Just a few simple flowers were then needed to complete this delightful design by Johann Obendrauf.

RIGHT AND INSET A decorative, soft-textured wool collar frames and complements the beautiful colours of the David Austin roses in this hand-tied design by Per Benjamin.

USEFUL PRODUCTS

Inspirational floral designers have at their fingertips knowledge of the products that make their designs possible. Most of these products are readily available online, by mail order and from craft shops worldwide.

They include:

- adhesives
- beads and buttons
- fibres and fabric
- foam and foam products
- pins
- polystyrene
- reeds, cane and bark
- tubes and mini containers
- wire and wire products

Adhesives

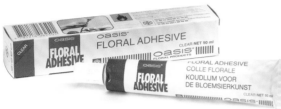

OASIS® Floral Glue

glue pot

spray adhesive

glue gun

double-sided tape

pot (anchor) tape

Beads and buttons

coloured beads

beads on decorative wire

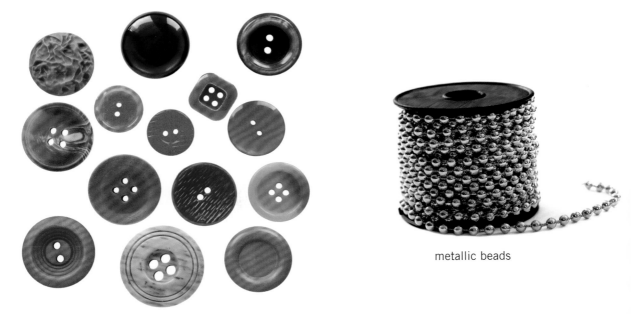

buttons

metallic beads

Fibres and fabric

raffia

sisal

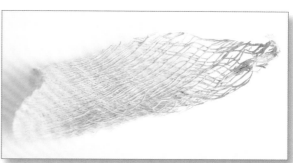

coconut fibre

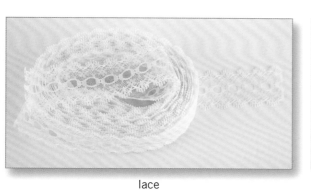

lace

ribbon

(from left) wired wool cord, wool and felted wool

twine

Foam and foam products

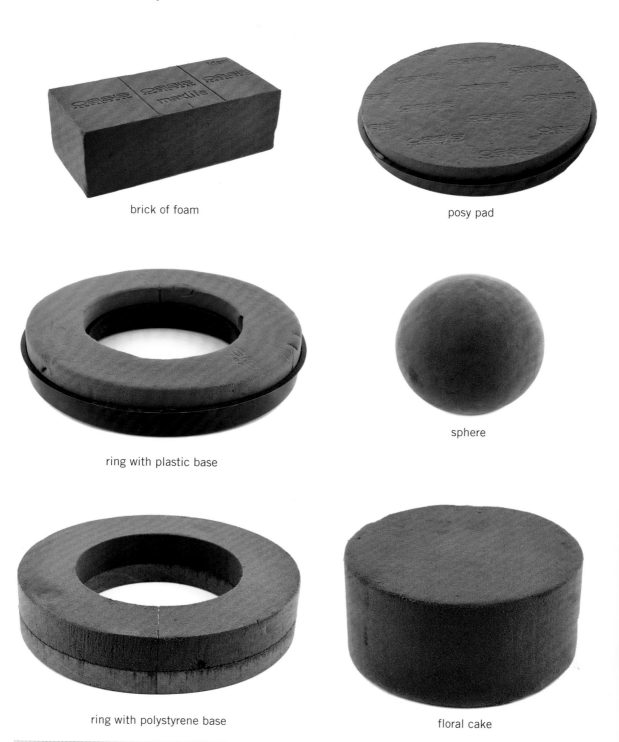

brick of foam

posy pad

ring with plastic base

sphere

ring with polystyrene base

floral cake

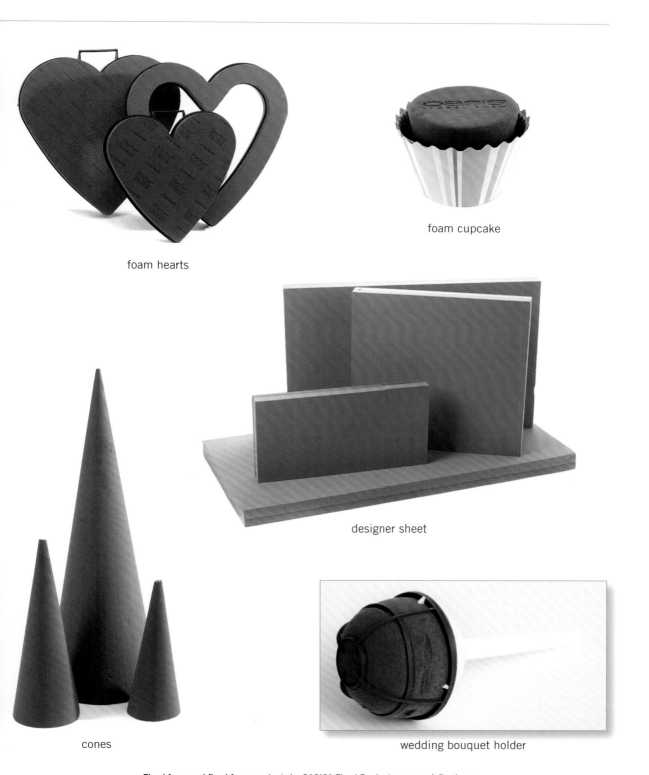

foam hearts

foam cupcake

designer sheet

cones

wedding bouquet holder

Floral foam and floral foam products by OASIS® Floral Products www.oasisfloral.com

Pins

decorative pins

German pins

Polystyrene

part of sheet

sphere

hemisphere

Reeds, cane and bark

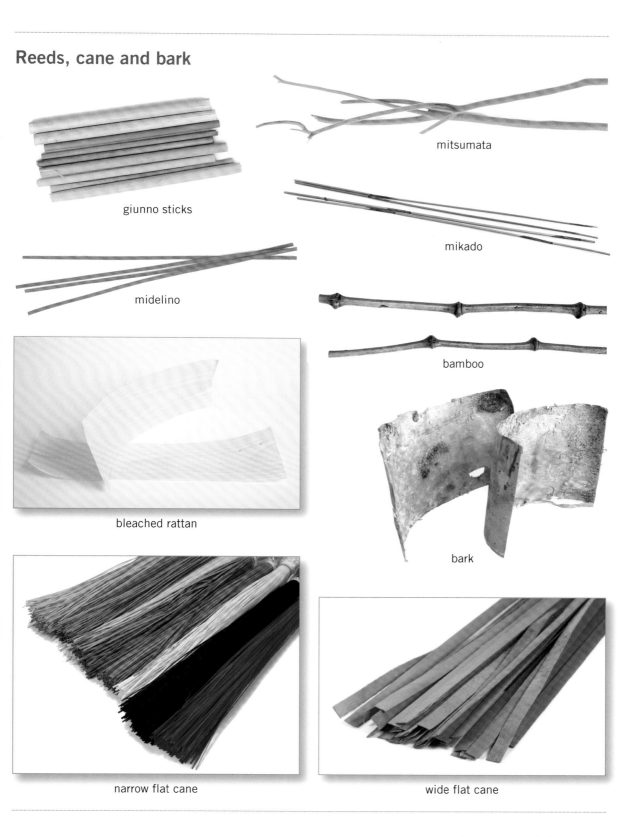

giunno sticks

mitsumata

mikado

midelino

bamboo

bleached rattan

bark

narrow flat cane

wide flat cane

Tubes and mini containers

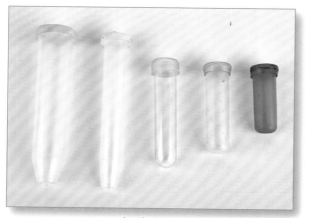

plastic tubes

glass tube (left) and perspex tube (right)

glass cone

light-bulb container

mini milk bottle

mini glass round bowl

glass seahorse

Wire and wire products

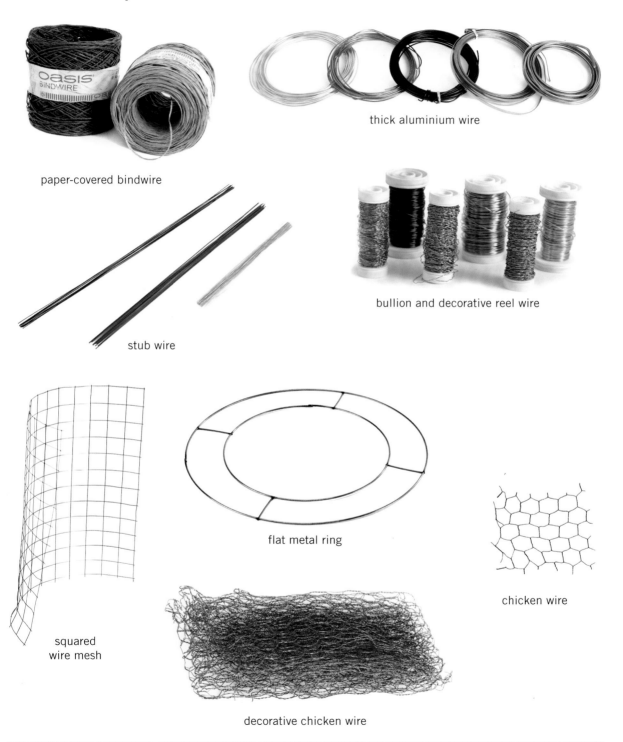

paper-covered bindwire

thick aluminium wire

stub wire

bullion and decorative reel wire

squared
wire mesh

flat metal ring

decorative chicken wire

chicken wire

Other products

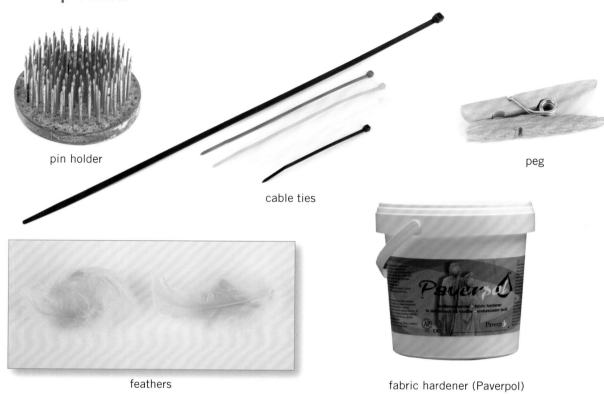

pin holder

cable ties

peg

feathers

fabric hardener (Paverpol)

shells

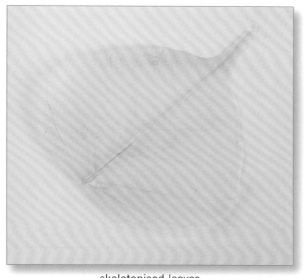

skeletonised leaves

preserved leaves
(*Stachys lanata*)

stones and pebbles

ACKNOWLEDGEMENTS

This book would not exist without the inspirational designs and generosity of all those whose work is featured, many of whom supported the events at Flowers@Chicheley and Flowers@Oxford. I have obtained permission and credited the vast majority of those concerned, but if I have unintentionally overlooked anybody please forgive me and let me know, so I can include you in the next edition.

I have been blessed with a team of wonderful helpers. The photographers have all created superb work. I would like to thank in particular Thomas de Hoghton, Chris Harten and Oliver Gordon. I must mention *The Flower Arranger* magazine published by NAFAS who have allowed me to use several images to illustrate specific techniques. Also Lieven Hemschoote, publisher of *Fleur Creatif*, who allowed me to take photographs at the event his company organizes in Bruges entitled 'Winter Moments'.

Yet again, Christina Curtis' invaluable botanical knowledge has been essential. Amanda Hawkes, the designer of my books, has once again found a way to present the information and images so that they both inform and inspire. Lesley Levene is a proof-reader par excellence and I always marvel at her skill. I owe a great debt of gratitude to Tim Harris, manager of The Flower Press for his constant and ready support.

Lastly, I must thank my family, friends and staff at the flower school for their forbearance, especially as this book goes to print the very day before my daughter Jane's wedding! At the flower school, a special thanks to Julia Harker for her painstaking monitoring of the images and designers and her enviable patience. Also to Tomasz Koson for setting up photo shoots, prepping flowers and helping me create designs at the last moment so that the book is fully comprehensive. I am proud that my teachers Neil Bain, Lynne Dallas, Dawn Jennings, Larry Walshe and Marco Wamelink have work included in this volume.

FLORAL DESIGNERS

I would like to thank all the inspirational floral designers whose work appears in this book. It could not have been written without them.

Abou, Maroun   376–377
Adriaenssens, Stef   217 (top), 230, 238, 241 (top), 281, 400–401, 402–403

Babar, Humaira   244–245
Bain, Neil   373
Baker, Margaret   384–385
Barber, Jacky; Ellis, Kathy; Hammond, Mavis   362 (top), 363
Barnes, Freda and Smith, Brenda   16–17
Bartholomé, Charlotte   270–271
Bates, Lana   46–47, 55, 61–62, 241, 261, 289, 340–341
Bates, Maureen   298–299
Bensley, Pip   368
Benjamin, Per   131, 155, 312, 313, 317, 357, 412–413
Berrill, Lee   93
Blacklock, Judith   12, 14, 27 (top), 103, 107, 158, 174, 179, 189, 208 (bottom), 292–3, 302 (top)
Blake, Adrienne   342 (bottom)
BluBelle Creative by Helen Curtis   308, 331, 379
Boet, Suzanne; Ferguson, Pam; London, Brenda; Swain, Ann   302 (bottom)
Bullock, Craig   383

Callebaut, Wim   143
Casati, Rudy   40–41, 108–109, 138, 184, 282–283, 406–407
Chihuly, Dale   133
Collier, Barbara; Hind, Mo; Parsons, Wendy; Temple, Maggie   157, 188
Coulton, Ann   89
Curtis, Christina   85, 218 (bottom), 219, 221, 342 (top), 358

Dallas, Lynne   11, 25, 59 (bottom), 160–161, 182, 297, 336
Dalsace, Marie-Noëlle   186–187, 246 (bottom)
Danthine, Marie Rose   122–123
De Houwer, Tom   102, 106, 199, 212, 251, 259
De Meulemeester, Jamie   364 (bottom)

De Ridder, Jan   69, 176–177, 255
Decoster, Vera   284
Duarte, Bruno   35, 234–235, 236, 277, 316
Duchateau, Annemie and Kruzslicz, Ferenc   135
Duffill, Mo   217 (bottom)

Edmonds, Jayne   337
Enel, Michele and Maccari, Muriel   34 (bottom)
Erema, Ioachim   74, 136 (top), 181, 190, 386–387

Ferchland, Oliver   77, 126–127, 128, 224, 228, 229, 328–329
Ferraro, Guiseppe   72, 100
Flower Council of Holland   48, 49, 80–81, 146–147, 292, 305, 306, 332–333, 344
Fontanillas, Carles   83, 197, 263, 314
Föhl, Julia and Koson, Tomasz   389
Freeman, Jenny and Ackroyd, Annette   243 (top)

Geiling–Rasmus, Felix   62, 175, 262, 278, 309
Goff, Lily   290–291

Hart, Anne and Lanning, Dolores   365 (top)
Hirayama, Makie   222, 243 (bottom)
Hodge, Tom   87
Hunt, Barbara and Preston, Maureen   156
Huyghe, Tania   233

Jakobsen, Jens   215
Jennings, Dawn   378 (top)

Kneepkens, Dennis   26, 191, 295, 324
Koene, Robert   15, 29, 33, 43, 45, 232, 254, 366
Koh, Damien   82
Koson, Tomasz   34 (top), 42, 200, 208 (top)

Laer, Sören Van and Verheyden, Greet   318–319
Leong, Laura   98, 99, 334, 338
Leong, Solomon   203, 223, 240, 303, 304, 362 (bottom)
LEHNER Wolle[3]   120, 130
Lersch, Gregor   58, 166, 180 (right), 404–405

Maddelein, Stijn   145, 180 (left), 315 (bottom)
Malyuchenko, Sergey   129, 310–311, 375
Massie, Joe   63, 112–113, 345
McSheehy, Margaret; Parsons, Wendy;
    Temple, Maggie   167
McSheehy, Margaret and Parsons, Wendy   388
Merryfield, Angela   38, 64–65, 144 (bottom), 356
Moerman, Yves   139
Mommen, Martine; Milissen, Luc; Palmaers, Chiel
    Vanclee en Ilse   94–95
Moseley, Jonathan   117
Moyses Stevens   27 (bottom), 330
Mullèr, Michel   335

Nash, David   393, 394–395
Nuffelen, Robin Van   408–409
Nummy, Cherie   231

Obendrauf, Johann   410–411
Obendrauf, Johann for LEHNER Wolle[3]   119
Oldenhof, Erika   88 (top)
Overputte, Damien   76

Pampling, Mark   213, 359 (right)
Pattyn, Geert   51, 132, 300
Penno, Alison   343, 355 (right)
Perez, Laurence   285
Perez, Laurence and Vitti, Martine   218 (top), 326
Petit, Clement   307
Phillips, Sue and Pampling, Mark for
    Fusion Flowers   213, 301, 399
Picca, Giuseppe   56–57, 140–141
Plattel, Rob   39, 84 (bottom), 88 (bottom), 124,
    183, 265–266–267, 369

Reeve, Jean and Patterson, Jane   125

Sakalova, Natalia   201
Simaeys, Stijn   13, 78, 96–97, 104–105, 116,
    159, 168–169, 178, 214, 225, 252, 253,
    258 (bottom), 260, 268, 272–273, 296,
    352–353, 359 (left), 371, 372, 390–391

SMITHERS-OASIS   134
Strain, Neill   18–19
Su, Lisi   360
Sumihara, Yoko   242
Sweden, Munkeröds   162–163

Taylor, Matthew and Cooper, Gary   30
ter Voorde, Miranda   70–71
Traigné, Marylène   121
Turangan, Ineke   294

Van Gansbeke, Rita   36–37, 84 (top), 320
Van Pamel, Frederiek   361
Vanden Berghe, Moniek   66, 73, 142, 144 (top),
    173, 264, 370, 392
Vanneste, Pieter   137
Vaughan, Mary Jane   148–149, 150–151, 327,
    346–347
Verkinderen, Lut   79, 185, 202, 237, 350–351,
    355 (left)
Vercoutere, Dieter   339
Verhelle, Hilde   111
Viaene, Hilde   110

Wacariu, Fabienne   59 (top)
Wakayama, Misako   210–211, 246 (top)
Walshe, Larry   24, 348–349
Wamelink, Marco   10, 67, 75, 196, 198 (bottom),
    206–207, 365 (bottom)
Watson, Jackie   68

2Dezign   50

PHOTOGRAPHIC CREDITS

Cappalunga, Marco 40–41
Cobley, Tony 342 (bottom), 343, 355 (right)

Bates, Lana 55, 61–62

Blacklock, Judith 23, 32, 62, 84 (top and bottom), 101, 133, 162, 165, 175, 208 (top), 215, 220, 239, 277, 307, 332, 364 (top), 365 (top), 367 (bottom), 378 (bottom)

De Hoghton, Thomas 11, 16–17, 34 (bottom), 36–37, 44, 59(top), 59(bottom), 79, 89, 110, 111, 116, 121, 122–123, 132, 137, 138, 139, 143, 158, 182, 185, 186–187, 201, 202, 210/211, 218 (top), 222, 233, 242, 243 (bottom), 246 (top), 246 (bottom), 253, 270–271, 272–273, 284, 285, 296, 297, 300, 320, 322–323, 326, 339, 350/351, 352–353, 354, 355 (left), 359 (left), 361, 364 (bottom), 367 (top), 370, 371, 383, 390–391

De Houwer, Tom 251
Dobbie, Lloyd 346–347
Draper, Johnny 243 (top)

Fetisov, Vasily 289
Flitman, Lev 46–47, 340–341
Flower Arranger, The 16, 31, 195, 342 (bottom), 362 (top), 363, 383
Flower Council of Holland 48, 49, 80–81, 146–147, 292, 305, 306, 332–333, 344
Fraser, Allen 393, 394
Freeman, Alex 24, 348–349

Goff, Lily 290–291

Gordon, Oliver front cover (slate background), 10, 13, 14, 15, 26, 27 (top), 28, 29, 30, 34 (top), 35, 39, 43, 56–57, 63, 68, 69, 70–71, 73, 78, 83, 85, 87, 88 (bottom), 93, 96–97, 98, 99, 102, 103, 104–105, 106, 114, 115, 129, 131, 135, 136 (bottom), 155, 156, 157, 159, 167, 168–169, 174, 176–177, 178, 184, 188, 190, 191, 197, 203, 204–205, 206–207, 209, 212, 213, 214, 223, 225, 226–227, 230, 231, 234–235, 236, 237, 240, 244–245, 247, 252, 255, 256–257, 258 (bottom), 259, 260, 261, 263, 265–266–267, 268, 277, 280 (right), 281, 298–299, 301, 302 (bottom), 303, 304, 312, 313, 314, 315 (top), 316, 317, 321, 324, 337, 345, 357, 360, 368, 369, 372, 374, 375, 376/377, 384–385, 386–387, 388, 389, 399, 402–403, 410–411, 412–413

Grüner, Andreas 77, 126–127, 128, 224, 228/229, 328/329

Harten, Chris 33, 45, 66, 72, 74, 82, 100, 108–109, 117, 119, 124, 125, 130, 136 (top), 140–141, 142, 145, 164, 166, 180 (left and right), 181, 183, 198 (top), 217 (top), 232, 238, 241 (top), 241 (bottom), 254, 262, 264, 269, 278, 280 (left), 310–311, 315 (bottom), 334, 338, 359 (right), 362 (bottom), 366, 400– 401, 406–407

Heath, Lucy 67, 198 (bottom), 325, 378 (top)

Ketz, Dominik 404–405
Khan, Lewis 42, 75, 160–161, 179, 200, 218 (bottom), 219, 221, 336, 342 (top), 358, 373

LEHNER Wolle[3] 120

Merryfield, Stephen 38, 64–65, 144 (bottom), 356
Mackenzie, Pippa 150–151
McCabe, Duncan 365 (bottom)

Nichols, Clive 12, 107
Nolegard, Pauline 27 (bottom), 330

Parker, Lyndon 217 (bottom)
Perego, Ignazio 282–283
Portsmouth, Rebecca FMPA 148–149, 327
Press Association 293
PSGstudio (Fleur Creatif) 18, 51, 58, 76, 88 (top), 94–95, 173, 199, 294, 307, 318–319, 392, 408–409

Smith, Toby 189, 208 (bottom), 302 (top)
SMITHERS-OASIS 134
Steve Merryfield 38, 64–65, 144 (bottom), 356
Stubbe, Mick 295

Tooze, Howard 308, 331, 379

Winslow, Julien 112–113

Zandbergen, Wim 50

Photo library credits
© matka_Wariatka/Fotolia front cover (tulips)
© iStock.com/_Vilor 1
© Zina Seletskaya/Fotolia 4
© Tarzhanova/Fotolia.com 416 (buttons)
© juliyarom/Fotolia.com 416 (metallic wire)
© iStock.com/jfens 427

OTHER TITLES FROM THE FLOWER PRESS

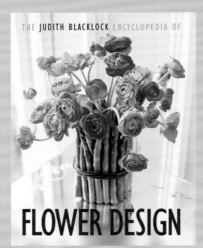

**The Judith Blacklock Encyclopedia
of Flower Design**
ISBN 978 0 9552391 0 6

**Flower Arranging
The complete guide for beginners**
ISBN 978 0 9552391 7 5

**Floristry
A step-by-step guide**
ISBN 978 0 9552391 5 1

Church Flowers
ISBN 978 0 9552391 6 8

TO ORDER

Order these books through any bookshop or online book retailer.
In the UK you can order direct from the publisher:
Tel: 01202 586848   www.selectps.com